What Happens When Women Say Yes to God

LYSA TERKEURST

HARVEST HOUSE PUBLISHERS
EUGENE, OREGON

Cover by Connie Gabbert

Interior design by Janelle Coury

Cover photo © Floral Deco / Shutterstock

WHAT HAPPENS WHEN WOMEN SAY YES TO GOD
Copyright © 2007 by Lysa TerKeurst
Published 2018 by Harvest House Publishers
Eugene, Oregon 97408
www.harvesthousepublishers.com

Library of Congress Cataloging-in-Publication Data
TerKeurst, Lysa.
What happens when women say yes to God / Lysa TerKeurst.
    p. cm.
Includes bibliographical references.
ISBN 978-0-7369-5048-0 (pbk.)
ISBN 978-0-7369-7261-1 (eBook)
    1. Obedience—Religious aspects—Christianity. 2. Christian women—Religious life. I. TerKeurst, Lysa. Radically obedient, radically blessed. II. Title.
BV4647.O2T47 2007
248.8'43—dc22
                                                                    2006030640

Printed in the United States of America

20 21 22 23 24 25 26 / VP-JC / 12 11 10 9 8

I dedicate this book to

Suzy Sandbo
and my other Long Island friends.

The day so many of you said yes to God
is one I will never forget.

Contents

A Soul That Longs for More

Whatever God says do, do it.

IT ALL STARTED THE DAY GOD told me to give away my Bible.

I was exhausted from traveling and speaking. All I wanted to do was to get to my assigned seat on the plane and settle in for a long winter's nap. Imagine my absolute delight at being the only person seated in my row. I was just about to close my eyes when two last-minute passengers made their way to my row and took their seats.

Reluctantly, I decided to forgo my nap. The last thing I needed was to fall asleep and snore or, worse yet, wake up with my head resting on the guy's shoulder beside me. No, I didn't need another most embarrassing moment, so I pulled a manuscript out of my bag and started reading.

"What are you working on?" the guy asked. I told him I was a writer and I was working on a book titled *Leading Women to the Heart of God.* He smiled and said he thought God was a very interesting topic. I agreed and asked him a few questions about his beliefs. Before long, I found myself reaching into my bag and pulling out my Bible, walking him through some key verses that dealt with the issues he was facing. He kept asking questions, and I kept praying God would give me answers.

All of a sudden, I felt God tugging at my heart to give this man my Bible. Now, this was not just any Bible. This was my everyday, highlighted, underlined, written in, and tearstained Bible. My kids had even drawn pictures in this Bible. I started to argue with God in my head, but His message was clear. I was to give away my Bible.

I emptied it of some old church bulletins and other papers, took a deep breath, sighed, and placed it in the man's hands. "I'd like for you to have my Bible," I said. Astonished, he started to hand it back to me, saying he couldn't possibly accept such a gift. "God told me to give it to you," I insisted. "Sometimes the God of the universe pauses in the midst of all His creation to touch the heart of one person. Today, He paused for you."

The man took my Bible and made two promises. First, he said he would read it, and, second, someday he would pass it on, doing for someone else what I'd done for him.

Before I knew it, the plane landed and we were saying our goodbyes. As I stepped into the aisle preparing to disembark, the woman on the other side of the businessman reached out and grabbed my arm. She'd been staring out the window the entire time we were flying, and I thought she'd been ignoring us. But her tearstained face told a different story. In a tone so hushed I could barely hear her, she whispered, "Thank you. What you shared today has changed my life." I put my hand on hers and whispered back, "You're welcome." Then a knot caught in my throat as tears welled up in my eyes. I didn't have another Bible to give away, so I gave her one of my books and hugged her goodbye. It has been said that we are to tell the whole world about Jesus, using words only if necessary. I saw this powerful truth come to life. Though I never spoke to this lady about Jesus, she saw Him through my obedience. How humbling. How profound.

As I got off the plane that day, I could barely hold back my tears. Three people's hearts were radically changed. I believe the businessman came to know Jesus as His Lord and Savior. I believe the same is true for the lady. But my heart was changed in a dramatic way as well. While on the one hand I was overjoyed at what God had done, I was also brokenhearted by the flood of thoughts that came to mind recounting times I'd told God no. How tragic to miss God's divine appointments. I just kept wondering, *How many times have I told You no, God? How many times because I was too tired, too insecure, too uncertain, too busy, or too selfish have I walked right past Your divine appointment for me and missed experiencing You?* I lifted up my heart to the Lord and whispered, "Please forgive me for all those noes. Right now I say yes, Lord. I say yes to You before I even know what You might ask me to do. I simply want You to see a yes-heart in me."

Several minutes after exiting the plane, I was weaving in and out of the crowds, trying to find my connecting gate, when I spotted the businessman again. He stopped me to tell me he had been praying to God and thanking Him for what happened on the plane. We swapped business cards, and, though we lived several states apart, I knew we would stay in touch.

About a month later he called to tell me his life had totally changed. He'd taken a week off from work to read the Bible, and he'd already shared his testimony with numerous people. When he said this to me, my mouth dropped open. I couldn't bring myself to tell him that I'd never taken a week off from work to read the Bible. God was definitely pursuing this man in a serious way! When I asked him what his favorite verse was, he said it was Proverbs 3:5-6: "Trust in the LORD with all your heart; and lean not on your own understanding; in all your ways acknowledge him, and he will make your paths straight." I thought to myself, *Wow! Look at how God has already answered that for my new friend.*

He also told me that after reading the Scriptures he knew he needed to get involved in a church, so he'd decided to visit a large church in his town. On his way there he passed another church, and a strong feeling came over him to turn his car around and go back to that church. So he did. When he got to his seat in the sanctuary, he opened up his bulletin and gasped. Inside the bulletin he saw my picture and an announcement that I was to be the speaker at an upcoming women's conference. He said he felt as though, once again, God had paused just for him.

That day on the plane, when God impressed on my heart to give this man my Bible, I did not know what would happen. This man might have thrown my Bible into the nearest airport trash can, for all I knew. Normally, I would have come up with a hundred reasons *not* to give my Bible away, but that day something changed in me. That day, for the first time, I truly heard the call of a woman who says yes to God: "Whatever God says do, do it."

A Fresh Invitation

When I said yes that day, I caught a glimpse of eternity. I saw how beautiful it is when God says to do something and it is done. And I thought, *Why wait for heaven? Why not say yes to God on this side of eternity?*

Oh, dear friend, the call to become a woman who says yes to God is the fresh invitation your soul is looking for. We all feel a tug at our heart and a stirring in our soul for more, but we are often afraid to venture past our comfort zone. Outside our comfort zone, though, is where we experience the true awesomeness of God.

I think at this point it is important for me to paint an accurate picture of what my life looks like on a daily basis. Lest you imagine me as this women dressed in sackcloth who is perfectly calm, amazingly

When I said yes that day,
I caught a glimpse of eternity.
I saw how beautiful it is when
God says to do something and it is done.
And I thought, *Why wait for heaven?*
Why not say yes to God
on this side of eternity?

organized, incredibly disciplined, and who spends hours upon hours on her knees in solemn solitude before the Lord, let me assure you that's not how it is. I am a wife and busy mom of five who can often be found rushing from one carpool to the next. My to-do list rarely gets fully accomplished. My emotions have been known to run wild, and my patience can easily run thin. I get pushed to the limit by everyday aggravations, such as a summer's worth of pictures getting erased from my digital camera by a child who wasn't even supposed to be handling the camera. And a dog that I love dearly who insists on running away. And some important paperwork that should be in a file that has mysteriously sprouted wings and flown the coop!

Can you relate? Great! You are a woman perfectly equipped to say yes to Him. Notice that I did not say you are a perfect woman. But if you are in the thick of living with all that life throws at you and you simply whisper yes, you are equipped. "Yes, Lord. I want Your patience to invade my desire to fly off the handle." "Yes, Lord. I want Your perspective to keep my emotions in check." "Yes, Lord. I want Your provision so things don't seem so overwhelming." "Yes, Lord. I want Your courage to do what I feel You calling me to do." "Yes, Lord. I want and need more of You in every moment."

You don't need perfect circumstances to be a woman who says yes to God. You don't need the perfect religious attitude or all the answers to religious questions. You simply have to surrender all that's clamoring for attention in your heart with the answer God is longing to hear spill from your lips: "Yes, God."

Each day when I wake up I pray a very simple prayer even before my feet hit the floor. *God, I want to see You. God, I want to hear You. God, I want to know You. God, I want to follow hard after You. And even before I know what I will face today, I say yes to You.* This simple act of surrender each morning will prepare your eyes to see Him, your ears to hear Him, your mind to perceive Him, and your heart to receive Him. This is how to live expecting to experience God.

You see, we have become so familiar with God yet so unaware of Him. We make the mysterious mundane. We construct careful reasons for our rules and sensible whys for our behavior. All the while our soul is longing for a richer experience—one that allows us to escape the limits of sight, sound, touch, taste, and smell and journey to a place of wild, wonder, and passion.

Women who say yes to God will see life like few others. They are drawn in and embraced by a love like no other. They don't have to wait until the next time they're in church to experience God because they sense God's presence all around them, all through their day. Instead of merely walking through the motions of life, they pursue the adventure of the moment-by-moment divine lessons and appointments God has in store for them. They *expect* to see God, to hear from Him, and to be absolutely filled by His peace and joy—and, therefore, they do and they are.

A woman who says yes to God isn't afraid to be honest with God. Just last week I woke up feeling drained and overwhelmed. I couldn't quite put my finger on the source of my anxiety, but I couldn't shake it, either. As I prayed my normal prayer of wanting to see and hear God, I told Him honestly that I really needed to see evidence of Him in my day. Later on I was in my kitchen washing dishes, preparing dinner, and talking with one of my sons. My attention was focused on my son while my hands were just going through the motions of my tasks. Suddenly I felt God's strong impression on my heart to look down in the sink before I reached for another dish. As I did, I saw a very sharp butcher knife sticking blade up from inside a glass. Immediately, I knew God's presence was there. I closed my eyes and thanked Him. More than just for sparing my hand from serious injury, I thanked Him for caring enough to be so real in my life.

A holy God in the middle of life's mundane activities will change your life. But you might not always feel happy about the changes. I can't let you think that being a woman who says yes to God means everything will suddenly be happily ever after. As I am writing this, I must tell you about an experience I had today where I simply wanted to throw my hands in the air, throw my computer out the window, and cry out to God, "You have hurt my feelings and I'm just a little unnerved and upset!"

I am on a retreat at a friend's lake house where I have three days during which I'd hoped to accomplish a lot of writing. I am under a tight deadline for this project and really needed to make a big dent in the task before me. Yesterday went great. I wrote almost 2000 words and the friends with me loved what I'd written. I went to bed excited about all I'd accomplished so far. Visions of a completed manuscript and my editor's praises danced in my dreams all night long. I woke up this morning ready to tackle another huge chunk of writing, but first I wanted to admire yesterday's accomplishment. I opened up my documents section and the manuscript was nowhere to be found.

Refusing to panic, I asked for my friends' help. They felt confident we could locate the document I'd saved three times the night before. After two hours of searching, one of my friends gently looked at me and verbalized the truth we'd all come to know. "It's gone, Lysa. You are going to have to start over."

Wait just a minute, I thought. *I have said yes to God today and had a great quiet time. I just know He can and will help me find this.* But for whatever reason, my document was gone and God had chosen not to bring it back. Tears filled my eyes as bitterness started to creep in my heart. Why would God allow this? My friend could sense my despair and gently replied, "Lysa, recently when something like this happened to me, someone told me to look at my loss as a sacrifice of praise to God. It is so hard in today's abundance to give God a true sacrifice, but losing 2000 words and a whole day's work would qualify. Give this to Him without feeling bitter."

I resisted slapping my well-meaning friend as she then broke into singing, "We bring a sacrifice of praise into the house of the Lord…" By the second stanza I actually found myself joining in with a lighter heart and a resilient spirit. Being a woman who says yes to God means making the choice to trust Him even when you can't understand why He requires some of the things He does. It also means that once you've said yes to God, you refuse to turn back, even when things get hard.

This kind of obedience invites you to embrace a bigger vision for your life. When you look at your everyday circumstances through the lens of God's perspective, everything changes. You come to realize that God uses each circumstance, each person who crosses your path, and each encounter you have with Him as a divine appointment. Each day counts, and every action and reaction matters. God absolutely loves to take ordinary people and do extraordinary things in them, through them, and with them.

A Party in Your Honor

Imagine you're planning a wonderful surprise party for someone you dearly love. You've made the plans, invited all the guests, and decided on an exquisite menu. You can't wait for the big moment when all the guests yell, "Surprise!" and your loved one finally joins in the festivities. You know she'll understand just how cherished and adored she is when she sees everything that's been done in her honor.

Finally, the time for the surprise arrives. All of the guests are waiting in anticipation at the front door. You see your loved one pull into the driveway, and you hear the car engine turn off. As she opens the car door, you see the interior lights come on while she gathers her things. Your heart races as you see her heading up the driveway. Suddenly, she makes an unusual turn and heads to the back door.

You quickly make your way to the back door to redirect her. Your cheerful greeting is met with a halfhearted smile, and your attempts to send her to the front door are brushed aside. She insists she is tired and will look at what you want to show her tomorrow. Only you know that tomorrow the guests will be gone, the leftover food will be stored away, and the party will be over.

How sad for the guest of honor who missed her own surprise party! And how disappointing for the party planner who orchestrated the event.

God must feel the same way when we miss the "surprise parties" (the divine appointments) that await us each day. How it must disappoint Him when we don't hear or don't listen to Him redirecting us to the front door. How it must grieve Him when we walk through our lives oblivious of His activity all around us. How it must break His heart when we brush aside something that not only would make us feel special and noticed by God, but also would allow us to join Him in making life a little sweeter for others.

How many times have we missed our own surprise party?

God reveals Himself and His activity to all of us, but very few really want an encounter with Him. Encounters cause extreme changes in our plans, our perspectives, and our personhood, and most of us hate change. In reality, though, the very act of trying to protect ourselves from change is the very thing that makes our life the boring mess that it sometimes is.

As I've traveled around the country speaking at conferences, I am amazed and saddened by the number of people missing out on the most exciting part of being a Christian—experiencing God. Over and over people tell me they want something more in their Christian life. They want the kind of relationship with God where they recognize His voice, live in expectation of His activity, and embrace a life totally sold out for Him. I suspect that tucked in the corner of your heart is the same desire. And I've discovered that the key to having this kind of incredible adventure is radical obedience.

The Road That Leads to Blessing

You may be surprised to discover that radical obedience is not really that radical. It is really biblical obedience—but we've strayed so far from biblical obedience that it now seems radical. In today's society, it is radical to obey God's commands, listen to the Holy Spirit's convictions, and walk in Jesus' character. But we will never experience the radical blessings God has in store for us without radical obedience. It is the road that leads to blessing. It is what happens when women say yes to God.

And you won't find the full blessing until you give walking in obedience your full attention. Obedience, however, is more than just "not sinning." It is having the overwhelming desire to walk in the center of God's will at every moment. Don't stumble over fearing you won't be perfect or that you are sure to mess up. Saying yes to God isn't about perfect performance, but rather perfect surrender to the Lord day by day. Your obedience becomes radical the minute this desire turns into real action. Radical obedience is hearing from God, feeling His nudges, participating in His activity, and experiencing His blessings in ways few people ever do.

If this is what you want, read on.

Six Simple Words

After hearing about the day I gave away my Bible, people often ask me if I've ever gotten it back. I always chuckle because, to be honest, I don't want to get that Bible back (or any of the Bibles I've given away since then)—at least not for a very long time. I've had this vision of one day being on a plane when I'm old and gray, and the person next to me starts talking. She tells me of the amazing things God has done in her life since the day she received a Bible from a stranger who had received it from another stranger who had received it from another stranger.

Saying yes to God
isn't about perfect performance,
but rather perfect surrender
to the Lord day by day.
Your obedience becomes radical
the minute this desire
turns into real action.

She'll then reach inside her bag and pull out a worn and tattered book I've held once before. Wow, what a day that will be!

The man I gave the Bible to that day has continued to share his testimony, and I still hear from others whose lives have been changed because of his story. Recently, a lady wrote to tell me that the "Bible man" opened up a business meeting she attended by sharing how God had changed his life.

> I just finished visiting with a friend of yours and mine. His name is Ron. Over the years I have seen him struggling with his success and the decisions in his life. Today, Ron is filled with a different spirit. Your actions brought him back in touch with God. He shared his story with the office on how he met you and the effect of your actions. Isn't it strange that we know God is powerful and we know that we should listen, but sometimes we shut Him out? I can't explain the emotion I felt when I heard this story, but I can tell you that I am seeking some way to be more active in spreading God's Word. Bless you and bless Ron for being wonderful messengers.

Don't we all long to see God at work? Evidence of His activity around us, in us, and through us is the greatest adventure there is. The God of the universe wants to use you!

There is but one requirement for this adventure. We have to set *our* rules and agendas aside—our dos and don'ts, our social graces and proper places—and follow God's command. His one requirement is so simple and yet so profound: *Whatever God says do, do it.* That's it. That is the entire Bible, Old Testament and New, hundreds of pages, thousands of verses, all wrapped up in six words.

It is the call of the radically obedient woman who makes the choice to say yes to God.

Bible Study

Did the story about the man on the airplane and giving him the Bible inspire you? How?

What is holding you back from going deeper in your relationship with God?

- Time?
- Intimidation?
- Not feeling like the Bible applies to your everyday life?
- Seems too hard?

Comment on one or more of the above or another thing you sense holding you back.

Psalm 19:7-10 (MSG) says:

> The revelation of GOD is whole and pulls our lives together. The signposts of GOD are clear and point out the right road. The life-maps of GOD are right, showing the way to joy. The directions of GOD are plain and easy on the eyes. GOD's reputation is twenty-four-carat gold, with a lifetime guarantee. The decisions of GOD are accurate down to the nth degree. God's Word is better than a diamond, better than a diamond set between emeralds. You'll like it better than strawberries in spring, better than red, ripe strawberries.

List what Psalm 19:7-10 from *The Message* promises about God's Word.

The resolve of the human spirit is truly an amazing thing. We will fight to the death for something we want to protect, truly believe in, or desire. So why would we be lackadaisical about the most eternally significant relationship there is?

Read Deuteronomy 6:5.

- How can you love God with your heart?
- How can you love God with your soul?
- How can you love God with your strength?

Is there something you might need to let go of in order to have the freedom to say yes to God?

- Fear that it may cost you too much?
- Uncertain that you will like what a life sold out to Christ looks like?
- Feeling insecure that you'll be able to go the distance?

Psalm 16:7-9 (NLT) says,

> I will bless the LORD who guides me; even at night my heart instructs me. I know the LORD is always with me. I will not be shaken, for he is right beside me. No wonder my heart is filled with joy, and my mouth shouts his praises! My body rests in safety.

Write below how this verse gives a sure answer for each concern listed above:

In this chapter we read, "Being a woman who says yes to God means making the choice to trust Him even when you can't understand why He requires some of the things He does. It also means that once you've said yes to God, you refuse to turn back even when things get hard."

Write out a personal prayer of commitment for your new adventure with God:

Hearing God's Voice

God wants us to live
in expectation of hearing from Him.

I RECEIVED THIS LETTER from Neil in the British Isles.

Dear Lysa,

It's winter in the U.K. My wife bought me an exercise bike for my forty-ninth birthday so I could commit to getting my weight down.

While I pedal, I turn on U.C.B. Europe radio [the Christian radio broadcast]. One morning I caught the final part of your story about the Bible man and the plane journey. I just wept right on through. The program repeats in the evening, so I taped it and listened to it again with my wife, and we both wept.

In the 26 years I've claimed to be a Christian, I think my witness has deteriorated. Your message has inspired me to try again. I realize that the time is short and the Lord is coming.

The man who delivers my coal knocked at the door today. He has been sick for several weeks, and he is only 42. I asked him what the problem had been. He has a brain hemorrhage. He went on to tell me that it had made him think about life. I asked him if he had a faith, but he didn't answer. So I shared briefly. It was off the cuff, but next week I'll be "preprayered" for him.

I've decided I will try to hear God's promptings and remember my time is not my own.

Every day, God speaks to us. Sometimes He invites us to draw close and listen as He reveals Himself, His character, and His direction. Other times He calls to us to participate in His purposes—for example, Neil sharing with the man who delivers his coal. Still other times He simply whispers to remind us of His amazing love for us.

Oh, what joy it is to know God speaks to me! But I've found that many believers are missing this vital element in their relationship with Him. As I've talked with people about my own radical obedience journey, they are quick to ask how they might hear from God too. Maybe you have some of these same questions: How do I know if God is speaking to me? How do I discern whether it is His voice speaking or just my own idea? What if I feel God is telling me to do something that doesn't seem to make sense?

There is no magic formula for being able to discern God's voice. We can *learn* to recognize it the way we recognize the voices of those close to us: by knowing Him. And when we know Him, we can tell if what we're feeling led to do is from Him or not.

I'll be honest. Though I hear from God all the time, I've never heard His voice audibly. When God speaks to me, it is a certain impression on my heart that I've come to recognize as Him. I've also learned to

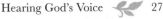

ask five key questions to help me determine if what I'm hearing is from God or not:

1. Does what I'm hearing line up with Scripture?
2. Is it consistent with God's character?
3. Is it being confirmed through messages I'm hearing at church or studying in my quiet times?
4. Is it beyond me?
5. Would it please God?

Asking these questions helps me tell the difference between my thoughts and God's impressions.

Does What I'm Hearing Line Up with Scripture?

God will not speak to us or tell us to do something that is contrary to His Word. But unless we know Scripture, we will not be able to discern whether what we are hearing is consistent or not with the Word. The apostle Paul wrote, "Do not conform any longer to the pattern of this world, but be transformed by the renewing of your mind. Then you will be able to test and approve what God's will is—his good, pleasing and perfect will" (Romans 12:2). God's Word is the language the Holy Spirit uses to help us understand what God is speaking to our hearts. We must get into God's Word and let God's Word get into us. This will transform our mind and prepare it for whatever God wants to tell us. Then, as Paul wrote, we will be able to test and approve not just God's good will, and not just His pleasing will, but His perfect will.

The good news is that you don't need a seminary degree to read your Bible. If reading God's Word is new for you, choose a translation that is easy to understand with a built-in commentary. A good rule of thumb is "Simply Start and Start Simply." Read a passage of Scripture

1. Does what I'm hearing
line up with Scripture?

2. Is it consistent with God's character?

3. Is it being confirmed through
messages I'm hearing at church or
studying in my quiet times?

4. Is it beyond me?

5. Would it please God?

and ask yourself: Who is this passage speaking to? What is it saying to me? What direction is this passage giving? How might I need to change my way of thinking or acting as a result of this verse? What are some other verses that relate to this topic, both in the Old Testament and New Testament?

These questions are just a starting place. I encourage you to get a journal and start recording the verses you study and some of your personal experiences with the things you are learning as you read God's Word.

Is What I'm Hearing Consistent with God's Character?

God's Word also provides rich information regarding His character. As you come across verses revealing aspects of God's nature, make note of them. Just as God always speaks in accordance with His Word, He speaks in accordance with His character. God will not say things that are inconsistent with who He is. The apostle Paul writes, "Those who live according to the sinful nature have their minds set on what that nature desires; but those who live in accordance with the Spirit have their minds set on what the Spirit desires" (Romans 8:5). What is it that God's Spirit desires? Answering this question helps us understand God's character.

We find great insight into God's character in Galatians 5:22-23: "The fruit of the Spirit is love, joy, peace, patience, kindness, goodness, faithfulness, gentleness and self-control." These characteristics in a person's life are the evidence of Christ at work. "The fruit of the Spirit is the spontaneous work of the Holy Spirit in us. The Spirit produces these character traits that are found in the nature of Christ. They are by-products of Christ's control—we can't obtain them by trying to get them without his help. If we want the fruit of the Spirit to grow in us, we must join our lives to his. We must know him, love him, remember him, and imitate him."[1] If the fruit of the Spirit is our imitation of Him, then it must be consistent with God's character.

When you feel God speaking to you, ask yourself: Is what I am hearing consistent with God's love, joy, peace, etc.?

In addition to the fruit of the Spirit, God's character is revealed in a loving relationship with us. As we experience God personally, we come to know new names for Him. When we've experienced His provision, we come to know Him as our Provider. When we've experienced His comfort, we come to know Him as our Comforter. When we've experienced His amazing love, we come to know Him as the Great Lover of our souls. The longer we know Him and the more we experience Him personally, the more we learn about His character.

If what you're hearing is consistent with God's character, ask the next question.

Is What I'm Hearing Being Confirmed Through Other Messages?

When God is speaking to me about a particular issue, I cannot escape it. Around every corner there is a sermon or Bible study lesson or speaker's topic or conversation with a friend that is consistent with what I've been hearing from God in my time alone with Him.

Do you spend time alone with God? We shouldn't wait to hear from God just on Sunday mornings or during a weekly Bible study or when a speaker comes to town. These are places to confirm what we've heard in our time alone, where we are personally studying God's Word, learning more about His character, and listening for His voice.

Think about having a conversation with another person. You both speak and you both listen. The same is true with our conversations with the Lord when we're one-on-one with Him. We shouldn't be doing all the talking. God wants us to pour out our hearts to Him, and then He wants to respond to us. Jesus shared this parable:

The watchman opens the gate for him, and the sheep listen to his voice. He calls his own sheep by name and leads them out. When he has brought out all his own, he goes on ahead of them, and his sheep follow him because they know his voice (John 10:3-4).

Now let's reread this verse with some clarifying remarks added in.

The watchman [Jesus] opens the gate [a way for us to have direct communication with God] for him, and the sheep [you and I] listen to his voice. He [God] calls his own sheep by name [He speaks to us personally] and leads them out [providing us with direction]. When he has brought out all his own, he goes on ahead of them, and his sheep follow him because they know his voice [they know his voice because they have spent time with him] (John 10:3-4).

Jesus is the one who provides a way for us to be able to talk with God and hear from God. God calls us by name. He wants to have a personal connection with each of us. Think about when you call someone's name. You know that person. You are calling on them so the two of you can connect in some way. This verse is telling us that the way God wants to connect with us is to provide direction for us in life. He has gone before us and sees the dangers and trials we will face. He is telling us the way to go, the perspectives to keep, the things to avoid, and the things to hold fast to. Most of all He is speaking to us because we are His own and He wants a relationship with us. He loves us, adores us, treasures us, and has a good plan for us. He longs for us to know His voice and listen to His voice. The only way to know and trust God in this way is to spend time with Him.

As a parent, I expect the same thing from my children. I know things they don't, and I can perceive dangers they are oblivious to. I want them to listen to me, but not because I want to exert a sense of authority in their life and simply boss them around. No, I want them to listen because I love them, adore them, treasure them, and want only the best for them. Even when they don't understand the why behind my instructions or like the limitations I put in place, I want them to be obedient because they trust me and they love me. The same is true in our relationship with our heavenly Parent.

When we invest in spending time alone with God, He will speak to us, and what we hear from Him in these quiet times will be echoed in other places. Listen for God's voice and then look for the message to be confirmed. If it is, you're ready to ask the fourth question.

Is What I'm Hearing Beyond Me?

When God leads or prompts us to do something small, we will be able to do it if we're willing. But sometimes God calls us to do something big that we feel we can't do in our own strength—either it is beyond our ability or beyond our natural human desire. It is not something we can strategize and manipulate into being in and of ourselves. It can only happen by God's divine intervention. The beauty of doing things beyond ourselves is that we will know it was by God's doing and His alone. And to Him we give all the glory.

I remember when God called me to write my first book. It seemed so exciting and thrilling to think of accomplishing this huge life goal. I envisioned the cover with my name on it. I delighted in imagining the first time I would walk into a bookstore and quietly say to myself, *I wrote that.* The excitement carried me through writing the first 10,000 words. Everything was clicking right along...until I got a note from my editor after she read my first installment. Her two-page, single-spaced feedback can be summed up in two shocking words, "Start over."

I got down on the floor beside my desk, buried my face into the carpet, and cried. "I can't do this, God. I can't write a whole book. What was I thinking? I'm not an author. I'm an imposter who somehow got lucky enough to fool this publisher with my proposal. But now they've seen the real me and think I'm a fool."

Did you notice an often-repeated word in my cries to God. "I'm not." "I can't." "I'm a fool." It was all about me and my inadequacies until I turned the statements into "God is." "God can." "God has called me; therefore, I am equipped."

If God is calling you to do something you feel is beyond you, you are in good company. God has a history of calling people to things that were beyond themselves. Pastor Rick Warren put it this way:

> Abraham was old, Jacob was insecure, Leah was unattractive, Joseph was abused, Moses stuttered, Gideon was poor, Samson was codependent, Rahab was immoral, David had an affair and all kinds of family problems, Elijah was suicidal, Jeremiah was depressed, Jonah was reluctant, Naomi was a widow, John the Baptist was eccentric to say the least, Peter was impulsive and hot-tempered, Martha worried a lot, the Samaritan woman had several failed marriages, Zachaeus was unpopular, Thomas had doubts, Paul had poor health, and Timothy was timid. That's quite a group of misfits, but God used each of them in his service. He will use you too.[2]

Don't look at your inabilities and dwell in insecurities. Look at the Almighty God. See this call as the opportunity to watch Him work in you and through you. If you answer yes to the question *Is this beyond me?* chances are God is speaking.

Would What I'm Hearing Please God?

It's easy to talk ourselves out of thinking we've heard from God. I think we'll pretty much use any excuse to convince ourselves it's not His voice so we don't need to act. But there's one very important question to ask when we feel prompted to do something, one question that takes away our excuses: Would this please God? You see, if what you are doing pleases God, then even if what you thought you heard from Him wasn't His voice, you still please Him. We should always seek to err on the side of pleasing God. Ask this question, and you'll know what to do.

These five questions are your starting place. The more you practice listening for God's voice, the more it becomes a natural part of your daily life. And here's the best news of all: God *wants* you to hear Him. He wants your faith to grow. He's told us so over and over in Scripture.

> This is my prayer: that your love may abound more and more in knowledge and depth of insight (Philippians 1:9).

> This is to my Father's glory, that you bear much fruit, showing yourselves to be my disciples (John 15:8).

> We ought always to thank God for you, brothers, and rightly so, because your faith is growing more and more, and the love every one of you has for each other is increasing (2 Thessalonians 1:3).

> For this very reason, make every effort to add to your faith goodness; and to goodness, knowledge (2 Peter 1:5).

> Finally, brothers, we instructed you how to live in order to please God, as in fact you are living. Now we ask you and urge you in the Lord Jesus to do this more and more (1 Thessalonians 4:1).

Living Out the Five-Question Filter

My conversations with God are more than a spiritual exercise for me. They are a lifeline. Growing up in my early childhood, I did not have a daddy who was very involved in my life. I was desperate to know that I was loved. I remember watching other little girls with their daddies and wondering what was so wrong with me that my daddy didn't adore me the way theirs did. Maybe it was because I wasn't pretty enough. Maybe I wasn't smart enough. Maybe he had never wanted me.

I was blessed to have another man adopt me as his own when my mom remarried. Charles has been a wonderful father to me who has loved me as his own. However, not having my biological father's love and acceptance left a hole in my heart. Often a little girl's sense of self-worth will be based on her father's love. And her opinion of God will often be based on her opinion of her earthly father.

Both of these were skewed for me. My sense of self-worth was severely lacking. I defined myself as an unwanted, unlovely, throw-away person. I viewed God as a distant, cold ruler who had somehow deemed me unworthy. Many years into my adult life, I came to see a different picture of God. He wooed me and loved me to a place where I finally surrendered my heart to Him. Then a miracle happened...He redefined my identity.

I was no longer a throwaway child. I was a holy and dearly loved daughter of the Most High King. I truly became a brand-new creation. I found the love and acceptance that had been so lacking in my early childhood. That little girl in me craved to spend time with the daddy I had missed out on for so long. He whispered to my heart that I was pretty and special and smart, and, best of all, that I was loved.

As a result of knowing what it feels like to be abandoned as a child, I have always had a tender place in my heart for the orphaned child. But after having three biological daughters of my own, I brushed aside any notion of adopting. That was until one unsuspecting day when God connected my family with two teenage boys from the war-torn country of Liberia, Africa. This meeting changed my family forever as God so clearly whispered to our hearts that they were to become part of our family.

As soon as I heard His whisper, my mind raced through the five-question filter.

1. Does what I'm hearing line up with Scripture?
2. Is it consistent with God's character?
3. Is it being confirmed through messages I'm hearing at church or studying in my quiet times?
4. Is it beyond me?
5. Would it please God?

God is very clear in Scripture that as Christians we are to take care of widows and orphans. Just a few weeks before meeting the boys I recorded the following verse in my journal: "Religion that God our Father accepts as pure and faultless is this: to look after orphans and widows in their distress and to keep oneself from being polluted by the world" (James 1:27). I had no idea why I was drawn to write this verse in my journal, but God knew. He made sure I was familiar with an answer to my first filter question. Yes, adopting the boys absolutely lined up with Scripture. And in the same verse God answered the second question. God defines part of His character as "God our Father." I saw that God had been a Father to me in my time of need, so I should be willing to be that for someone else in need.

The confirmations were also undeniable. God had been bringing friends into my life who had adopted orphaned children. I never thought it would be something my husband would be open to, and yet God drew his heart to a place of acceptance. My girls begged us to consider adopting and prayed often for big brothers. It seemed everywhere I turned the theme of adopting was staring me in the face. Sermons at church, verses in my quiet times, songs on the radio, and whispers by God to my heart all seemed to be saying the same thing. Yes, adopting these boys was being confirmed.

The fourth question did not require much thought at all. Yes, this was totally beyond me. Having boys was beyond me. I had grown up with all sisters and then had three daughters. I felt very ill-equipped to be a mom of boys—especially teenage boys. Having five kids was beyond me. My schedule was already crazy with three kids. How in the world would I be able to add two more? Financially, this seemed beyond what we could do. Not to mention the host of fears that flooded my brain. What if one of the boys hurt one of my girls or hurt me or had emotional baggage that would take a huge toll on the stability of our family? I would only be willing to do this if I knew beyond a shadow of a doubt that it was God's plan and not my own. Only in His strength would this be possible.

The last question became pivotal in our decision to pursue adopting the boys. More than anything else I desire to please God, but the pull of taking an easier path was incredible with this particular invitation. The tug of believing that my worst fears would surely be waiting on the other side of this step of obedience made me want to run and hide. But the love of God kept my heart stilled, and His constant reassurances kept me on course. We said yes to God, not because we were completely comfortable with adopting, but rather because we completely trusted Him.

His voice was strong and gentle, saying, "Do not fear. Remember how I faced the devil in the wilderness, and how I conquered with the sword of the Spirit, which is the word of God. You too have your quick answer for every fear that evil may present—an answer of faith and confidence in Me. Where possible, say it aloud. The spoken word has power. Look on every fear not as a weakness on your part due to illness or worry, but as a very real temptation to be attacked and overthrown. Does the way seem a stony one? Not one stone can impede your progress. Courage. Face the future, but face it only with a brave and happy heart. Do not seek to see it. You are robbing Faith of her sublime sweetness if you do this. Just know that all is well and that Faith, not seeing but believing, is what will bear you to safety over the stormy waters."[3]

So, we let faith carry us as we faced the future as courageously as we could. We quoted Scripture after Scripture and reminded God that this was His adventure that we were simply saying yes to while trusting

Him completely. And you know what we discovered? Sheer joy. Not in the circumstances that we faced necessarily, but in the absolute assurance that we were being obedient to God and walking in the very center of His will.

I can honestly tell you on the other side of this great adoption adventure that I can't imagine my life without my boys. I am so thankful that I followed God's perfect plan instead of being lured away by fear and worry. We've had our boys for three years now, and I'm more convinced than ever that even though they were not born from my body, they were born from my heart. Maybe that was the purpose of that place in my heart that seemed so much like a hole when I was younger, but now I see it as the channel through which God brought my boys home.

Use this five-question filter as a starting place in your conversations with God. Listening for God's voice and communicating with Him has not always come naturally to me. To this day I have to seek it by asking for the desire, discipline, discernment, direction, and delight. I ask for the desire to want God more than anything else. I ask for the discipline to make my relationship with Him top priority. I ask for the discernment to know the difference between my own thoughts and God's voice. I ask for clear direction at each crossroad in my life. I ask for my relationship with God to be characterized by sheer delight rather than a sense of duty. Have you ever asked God for this type of relationship with Him? When you ask for these things boldly and live in expectation of hearing from God, you will. In Jeremiah 29:13 God promises, "You will seek me and find me when you seek me with all your heart." Then respond by saying yes to Him and confidently walking in absolute dependence and glorious obedience.

Yes, indeed. I love being a woman who says yes to God.

Bible Study

Read Romans 12:1-2 in the NIV. Then, write out a definition for the following:

Living sacrifice:

Pleasing to God:

Do not conform:

The pattern of this world:

Transformed:

Renewing of your mind:

Test and approve God's will:

Now reread these verses and summarize what you can learn from them about discerning God's voice:

List some areas of your life that you currently honor God in:

List some areas that you sense you may need to sacrifice or change:

Are there areas of your life where you've conformed to the world's way of thinking?

How can you renew your mind in this area?

Find two Scripture verses that might be helpful to memorize as you seek to be renewed in this area. Write those here.

What is the promise from these verses for those who actively seek to be transformed and renewed in the way they think?

Write the five questions for discerning God's voice you learned in this chapter:

1.

2.

3.

4.

5.

Remember, this is not the end-all way for hearing God's voice. It is simply a starting place. Which of these questions do you find most challenging? Discuss this in your Bible study group. If you are not doing this as part of a group, find a Christian friend and spend some time discussing this and looking up Scriptures to help you better understand it.

In *The Message,* Romans 9:25-26 says, "Hosea put it well: I'll call nobodies and make them somebodies; I'll call the unloved and make them beloved. In the place where they yelled out, 'You're nobody!' they're calling you 'God's living children.'"

Paul continues,

> How can we sum this up? All those people who didn't seem interested in what God was doing actually embraced what God was doing as he straightened out their lives. And Israel, who seemed so interested in reading and talking about what God was doing, missed it. How could they miss it? Because instead of trusting God, they took over. They were absorbed in what they themselves were doing. They were so absorbed in their "God projects" that they didn't notice God right in front of them, like a huge rock in the middle of the road. And so they stumbled into him and went sprawling. Isaiah (again!) gives us the metaphor for pulling this together: Careful! I've put a huge stone on the road to Mount Zion, a stone you can't get around. But the stone is me! If you're looking for me, you'll find me on the way, not in the way (Romans 9:30-33 MSG).

What a perfect way to end our study—understanding that God wants us to live in expectation of hearing from Him. Sometimes we'll hear Him giving us direction or pointing us to a divine appointment. Other times we'll glean from Him wisdom, correction, or encouragement. But mostly I pray you'll hear His glorious voice proclaiming, "You are somebody! You are my chosen beloved!"

3

When Obedience Becomes Radical

God wants us to be willing to obey
with our whole heart.

I WAS ATTENDING a large conference where the speaker challenged us to pray and ask God to use us in an extraordinary way for His kingdom. Something stirred in my heart, and I started praying. When I got back to the hotel room that evening, I not only continued to pray for God to use me, but I wanted Him to show me what He required. I knew I couldn't climb to new heights in my spiritual journey without going into strict training to prepare. So I knelt beside my hotel bed and asked God to reveal to me what to do.

After I finished praying, I picked up the remote control to click on the evening news, and two words suddenly came to mind: radical obedience. *Radical obedience?* I questioned. *I'm obedient, Lord. I read my Bible, go to church, and try to be a good person.* Then something else came to my mind: Stop watching TV altogether and put your house up for sale.

What? I was stunned. *God, how do I know this is You speaking and not just a crazy notion in my head?*

One thing I did know—I was at a crossroads. I could brush these thoughts aside and say I didn't know for sure that this was God speaking to me, or I could heed His direction. I put down the remote and dropped to my knees once again. I wanted to do whatever He asked me to do, but I wasn't sure I could do this. I didn't doubt God. I doubted my ability to really know if God was speaking to me. I doubted my courage.

As I continued to pray, my mind was flooded with Scriptures that were consistent with what I felt God was calling me to do. Some of those powerful verses were 1 Peter 1:13-16:

> Prepare your mind for action; be self-controlled; set your hope fully on the grace given you when Jesus Christ is revealed. As obedient children, do not conform to the evil desires you had when you lived in ignorance. But just as he who called you is holy, so be holy in all you do; for it is written: "Be holy, because I am holy."

I decided it must be God I was hearing from and I should look for His confirmation over the next couple of weeks.

I also asked God why He'd chosen these two specific actions. After all, I wasn't a TV junkie, and our house didn't have us living beyond our means. As I prayed, I felt God telling me why the TV had to go. I enjoyed sitting down after a tiresome day and being entertained. God showed me that I was vulnerable and empty during those times. It wasn't that what I was watching was bad—it just wasn't God's best. I was filling myself with the world's perspectives and influences, while He wanted to be my strength and fill me with Himself. I knew it would be hard to break this habit, but I was determined to ask God for the strength to do so. I prayed that my desire to please Him would be stronger than my desire for television.

I hope you understand that I'm *not* saying all television is bad, and I'm not making a case here for all Christians to throw out their sets. What I am saying is that God wanted *my* obedience in this area for a certain season. I actually had felt His leading to turn off the TV before that night in the hotel room, but I had ignored Him and justified my disobedience to the point where God needed to get my attention. He wanted me to make a choice between my desire and His. I took a sabbatical from television for two and a half years. When I finally felt God giving me the freedom to turn it back on, something amazing had happened. I was no longer tied to it. I no longer felt the need to record programs I missed. I no longer had any must-see shows. I was able to objectively and carefully discern what would be good to watch and what wouldn't. I found that I was much more picky then I'd ever been before and a lot less willing to make compromises on what was questionable. God may not ask you to turn off the TV—He may ask you to do something else. The point here is that there may come a time at some point in your life when you will need to decide between your will and His.

One thing you can be assured of is that God has already worked out all the details of what your obedience will accomplish—and it is good. We need not fear what our obedience will cause to happen in our life. We should only fear what our *dis*obedience will cause us to miss. The sooner this truth resonates in your heart, the quicker you can make peace with a command from God that you don't fully understand. We tend to want to see the big picture complete with all the details before stepping out in obedience to God. We long for a cost analysis where we can weigh out what we'd be giving up against what we'd be gaining and then decide if the trade is worth it.

This is how I felt about God's request to sell our home. I kept think- ing, *My home is very precious to me. Not for its financial wealth, but for the wealth of memories we have made there. Why would God ask me to let this go?* I thought about the things we would not be able to take with us if the house sold: the door frame where we've measured each of our girls' growth since they were toddlers, the handprint tiles we made when we added a bathroom in the playroom, the Bible we'd buried in the foundation when we built the house. Small as they are, these things made our house our home. I decided I would wait for God's confirmation that we were really supposed to put the house on the market.

When I returned home from the conference, I was nervous about mentioning selling the house to my husband, Art, so I said very little. I just kept looking and listening for God's confirmation. Art had just completed construction on his dream bass pond and several landscaping projects. I asked God to reveal the perfect time to share my heart with my husband. A few days later we were both in our bedroom reading when Art looked up from his book and told me of the devotion he'd just studied.

"It had to do with the fact that sometimes we work so hard to make a heaven on earth that our hearts are pulled away from our real home with God," he said. Then he looked me straight in the eyes and added, "Lysa, I think we should sell our house."

I was shocked. But with tears in my eyes and God's confirmation in my heart, I told him I'd call a Realtor that very day.

When we got to the meeting with the real estate agent, she asked all kinds of questions about the house and our land. When the pond was mentioned, Art's eyes sparkled and he went into great detail about all he'd done to make it the perfect bass pond. He talked on and on about it, and even went so far as to say that while we wanted to be obedient to God in putting the house on the market, we really didn't want to try to aggressively sell it.

We left the meeting and headed home. When we reached the part of our driveway that curves around the pond, we were stunned by what we saw—82 dead fish floating in the water. We had never seen even one dead fish in our pond, so seeing 82 stopped us in our tracks. What followed was a scene I'll never forget. Art got out of the car and, with tears streaming down his cheeks, knelt beside the pond and asked for God's forgiveness. God had made His request clear, and we had given Him a halfhearted response.

A Whole and Purified Heart

God is not interested in half of our heart. He wants it all, and He wants to remove the things that stand in the way of that.

> "See, I will send my messenger, who will prepare the way before me. Then suddenly the Lord you are seeking will come to his temple; the messenger of the covenant, whom you desire, will come," says the Lord Almighty. But who can endure the day of his coming? Who can stand when he appears? For he will be like a refiner's fire or a launderer's soap. He will sit as a refiner and purifier of silver; he will purify the Levites and refine them like gold and silver (Malachi 3:1-3).

The messenger in this passage refers to John the Baptist. He would go before Jesus and prepare for Jesus' first coming. Now *we* are the messengers who are called to prepare people for Jesus' second coming. God wants to purify our whole heart so we are prepared and mature for our calling.

God turns up the heat from the refiner's fire so our impurities will rise to the top where they can be skimmed off and discarded. I appreciate the insight the *Life Application Study Bible* sheds on this passage:

> Without this heating and melting, there could be no purifying. As the impurities are skimmed off the top, the reflection of the worker appears in the smooth, pure surface. As we are purified by God, his reflection in our lives will become more and more clear to those around us. God says leaders (here the Levites) should be especially open to his purification process.[1]

Isn't it interesting that the Bible also tells us that the Levites' inheritance would not be land but rather God Himself (Numbers 18:20)? God wants us to desire Him above all else.

I didn't want to give God any more halfhearted answers. I was determined that when He spoke to my heart, He would never again have to shout. By asking Art and me to put our home up for sale, God was skimming greed from our hearts. Art and I were holding what God had given us with a closed fist. God wanted to teach us that when we tightly hold on to the things of this world, we not only lose the desire to give, but we lose the ability to receive more as well.

Did you catch that? If we hold all that we treasure with our hands open and our palms facing upward, we are telling God we recognize it is His and we offer it up freely to Him. God may or may not remove what we've offered Him, but He will continue to fill our open hands with blessings—His amazing blessings and not the cheap counterfeits of the world!

Offering It All to God

No one understands the concept of offering it all to God better than Abraham (Genesis 22). When God commanded Abraham to lay his only son on the altar of obedience, I am sure Abraham fully expected to plunge the dagger through Isaac. It would be an end…the death of a dream. Yet, Abraham was willing to give up the son he loved to the God who loved him more, and God blessed him. God poured His compassion and mercy into Abraham's open hands, and He spared Isaac. But even more than that, God lavished the evidence of His presence upon Abraham, and Abraham walked away having experienced God in a way few ever do. God wants to know if we're willing to give up what we love to Him who loves us more. He desires for us to open our fists and trust Him with absolutely everything.

As I opened my fist about our home, I felt God piercing a little

If we hold all that we treasure
with our hands open and
our palms facing upward,
we are telling God
we recognize it is His and
we offer it up freely to Him.

dark corner of my heart. My selfishness couldn't reflect God's generous heart. But as I let His light in, His reflection became clearer in my life. Then something amazing came about. Just as God provided a ram instead of taking Isaac, God did not allow our house to sell. For more than a year the Realtor's lockbox stayed on our front door as a beautiful reminder that we are managers and not owners of this home. Interestingly enough, the week we brought our boys home the box disappeared. Maybe the Realtor finally came and got it, or maybe God removed it to get our attention. But isn't the timing interesting?

I'm so thankful I made the connection between these two events so I could weather the transition of going from three to five children in a more settled way. I've always been a bit particular with my home. I like it to smell nice, sound quiet, and have a sense of order about it. Having three little girls who like to play quietly fit so nicely into my scope of how things should be. Then suddenly we had five children and things stopped being just so. It's not that any one of us is particularly messy or loud; it's just the nature of seven people living under the same roof.

There have been times where I admit to feeling bitterness and resentment creep into my heart toward my kids…all my kids. Every time I would clean something that ended up dirty just minutes later, I felt a little pang in my heart. Every time I went to look for an item in its assigned place and it had mysteriously disappeared, I felt this pang twist and grow. Every time I discovered something broken or destroyed, it felt as though the pang had grown into a choking vine in my throat. I found myself snapping at the kids and blaming them for anything and everything that went wrong at home.

I was in the middle of one of my aggravated dissertations one day when one of my sons stopped me and asked me the strangest question. "Mom, will you teach me to dance?"

I was mad and in no mood to dance. My thoughts were racing. *Dance? Dance? I am trying to teach you to put things back where they belong and stop messing up my house, and you want to dance?* Then my attention turned fully to him as he lifted out his hands, signaling he wanted to dance as if I were wearing a princess ball gown and he were wearing a tux. His gaze was so sincere that suddenly the missing scissors I had been so frustrated by no longer gnawed at my attention. Here was this beautiful young man awkwardly lifting up his arms and asking me to dance. This boy, who just months before had been stuck in a forgotten orphanage on the other side of the world with no hope and no reason to dance, was standing in my kitchen asking me to show him how.

I took his hand, wrapped my arm around his shoulder, and taught him to step and glide and twirl and dip. The world seemed to melt away as I realized what a privilege this experience was. How selfish of me to call our home "my house." How ungrateful I must have seemed to God. I could have a neat and tidy house where things never got lost, misplaced, or broken if there were no others living there but me. But my heart never wanted just a house. My heart longs for a home full of people who I love. As we stopped dancing, I lifted up a prayer of thanksgiving to God. I praised Him for teaching me to finally let go of my house so I could have a real home.

I no longer see things like this in my life as mere coincidence and brush them aside. I ponder these events and encounters. I pray over them. I pursue God and ask Him what I'm supposed to learn through the experience.

I suspect you have moments like this where God's fingerprints are all over them. Live in expectation of experiencing God and hearing His voice. Record these times in a journal. Look for answers to the prayers you've prayed and understanding from the steps of obedience God has called you to take. See how God weaves everything together in deep, wonderful, and wondrous ways.

Abiding in the Sweet Secret Place

Can I let you in on something? There is a place I escape to that allows my soul to breathe and rest and reflect. It is the place where I can drop the "yuck" the world hands me and trade it in for the fullness of God. It is a place that God reassures me, confirms that He has everything under control, and gives me a new filter through which I can process life. The Bible calls it the remaining place. I call it my sweet secret place.

John 15:4 says, "Remain in me, and I will remain in you. No branch can bear fruit by itself; it must remain in the vine. Neither can you bear fruit unless you remain in me." Let's be honest. It's hard for a well-meaning soul that desires radical obedience to God to live in a body made of flesh. Our flesh is pulled by the distractions of the world, lured to sell our soul for temporary pleasures, and conned by Satan's evil schemes. Other people rub us the wrong way, and we instantly want to give them a piece of our mind. Worldly wealth screams that if only you could do more to have more, then ultimate happiness could be yours. And our right to be right seems to supersede the sacrificial call of God. All the while God invites our souls to break away from the world and remain in Him.

To remain in Him and enter the secret place, I simply have to close my eyes and make the choice to be with God.

Sometimes it's because I'm in a desperate place. I pray, "God, I am here and I need You right now. I'm feeling attacked, invaded, pressed, and stressed. Meet me here and help me process what I'm facing using Your truth. Nothing more and nothing less. I don't want this thing I'm facing to be processed through my selfish and insecure flesh. I will surely act in a displeasing and dishonoring way if I'm left to face this on my own. Block my flesh's natural reaction and fill me with Your Spirit. You handle this for me. You speak what needs to be spoken and give power to hold my tongue for what needs to be left in silence."

Other times I need to be with God because I'm feeling pulled into something I know is not part of His best plan for me. I see something new I can't afford. How easy it is to justify our way to the checkout line, whip out a credit card, and decide to deal with the consequences later. Or maybe it is a relationship we know is not in God's will. Or a particular eating habit we know is not healthy for us.

Whatever it is, we don't have to be rendered powerless by this pull. We can pray, "God, I know You are more powerful than this pull I am feeling. I know this thing I think I want so much will only provide temporary pleasure. I know the consequences of making this choice will rob my joy and peace in the near future. Through Your power I am making the choice to walk away. I will find my delight in You and look forward to feeling Your fullness replace the emptiness this desire is creating."

Still other times I simply know I need a fresh filling of God's Spirit in me. I go to this secret place and simply talk to God. Then I listen for His voice. Sometimes He provides direction and instruction on something that needs to be done. Other times I sense Him warning me of something coming. Still other times He simply lavishes me with His love.

I love saying yes to God and going to the secret place with Him. God clearly tells us in John 15:4 that this is the only way to bear fruit in our lives. It is the only way to experience what Galatians 5:22-23 explains this fruit to be: love, joy, peace, patience, kindness, goodness, faithfulness, gentleness, and self-control. Oh, how I want these to be the character of my heart and the legacy of my life.

Obedience is the key that unlocks this secret place with God. John 15:10 goes on to explain this, "If you obey my commands, you will remain in my love." The more we say yes to God, the more we will live in expectation of seeing Him. The more we expect to see God, the more we will. The more you experience Him, the more you'll trust Him. The more you trust Him, the more you'll open up your hands in absolute obedience.

Obedience becomes radical when we say, "Yes, God, whatever You want," and mean it. We release our grip on all that we love and offer it back to Him, who loves us more. And it is into these upturned hands that God will pour out His blessings—His abundant, unexpected, radical blessings. Soon, saying yes to God will no longer be a discipline of your heart but rather the delight of your life.

We release our grip on
all that we love and offer it back to Him,
who loves us more.
And it is into these upturned hands
that God will pour out His blessings—
His abundant, unexpected, radical blessings.

Bible Study

Read Titus 2:11-12.

What are we to say no to?

Define this in the realm of your everyday life.

Titus 2:11-12 in *The Message* says,

> God's readiness to give and forgive is now public. Salvation's available for everyone! We're being shown how to turn our backs on a godless, indulgent life, and how to take on a God-filled, God-honoring life. This new life is starting right now, and is whetting our appetites for the glorious day when our great God and Savior, Jesus Christ, appears. He offered himself as a sacrifice to free us from a dark, rebellious life into this good, pure life, making us a people he can be proud of, energetic in goodness.

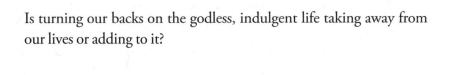

Is turning our backs on the godless, indulgent life taking away from our lives or adding to it?

What is it taking away? What is it adding?

Is there something that stirred in your heart as you read this chapter that God might be leading you to give up either permanently or for a season?

What is holding you back from doing this?

Comment on this statement from the chapter:

> "We need not fear what our obedience will cause to happen in our life. We should only fear what our *dis*obedience will cause us to miss."

Read Isaiah 41:13. Are we to give things up in our own strength? Are we walking this new path of deeper obedience alone?

How refreshing and comforting to know that God doesn't point us down this path of obedience and then simply stand back to watch us struggle. No, He takes our hand and leads us, whispers reassurances, and gives us back so much more than we give up.

In the chapter we read John 15:4. Record that verse here.

List the fruits found in the secret abiding place.

Of all these fruits, list three that you want to focus on when you escape to the secret place with God this week.

    1.

    2.

    3.

Now, look up Scriptures that give direction and instruction on pursuing these fruits and record them below.

Lastly, journal your thoughts below about this statement: "Soon, saying yes to God will no longer be a discipline of your heart but rather the delight of your life."

4

You Never Know How God Will Use You Until You Let Him

God must be Lord of all if He is our Lord at all.

I RECEIVED AN AMAZING letter from Christine in Colorado:

> Ever since I became a Christian in high school, the mark of my faith had always been radical obedience to Christ. I loved the church and everything about it, and I was always striving to follow Jesus beyond the everyday practicalities of faith. I was always certain there had to be more to Christianity than just Bible study, fellowship times, and prayer, and I found true joy in being involved in the lives around me.
>
> In the aftermath of September 11, though, I found myself with new questions, seeking God's true direction. I found myself disillusioned with the church and disenchanted with my faith. I heard you speak on radical obedience at a women's conference, and it was as though my heart was being called back to the roots of radical obedience.

As I celebrated my birthday the other week, I really had a chance to reflect on where God has been taking me over the past year. Has it ever been a wild ride! He has torn down all the things I had held so dearly about the church and about Christianity. And in the process, I am finding the Jesus I knew when I first became a Christian—the Jesus of social justice, mercy, and compassion. The Jesus who did not walk blindly through the earth and not feel the suffering of those around Him. He and the disciples were not tame and safe and nice. They were not a social club with watered down grace and entry requirements that have nothing to do with the sacred. They did not trade that which was eternal for that which was material.

At the same time, God has reawakened a heart of compassion and mercy in me. I am more aware than ever of the needs of others, and I have found great joy in working with social projects and even acts of compassion in everyday life. I see so much brokenness, so much pain in the lives of the women around me, and so often their cries are unheard and their needs go unnoticed as they walk alone through the trials of life. I have really been trying to reach out more to those around me and to draw them closer to the only One who holds the answers to life's questions.

Whether I'm writing an encouraging note to a discouraged friend or lending a helping hand to a mother who is overwhelmed with the responsibilities of her life, I've discovered it's so simple to bring the light of God into the midst of our everyday world. It is in the small acts of life that He can be reflected so beautifully—taking a meal to a new mother, welcoming a new neighbor with an invitation for dinner, or even just smiling at strangers as we pass them on the street. As I pause to help others, I am reminded that, just like Jesus, we are called to notice the people around us and to bring a touch of hope into their lives.

Looking back at where I've been, I can see now that I had gotten off track. I was caught up in the social club mentality that so often permeates the church, and I had lost sight of what was really important. Yet, out of my brokenness, I have seen the true call of Christ…a call to love our neighbors in ways that may seem radical in our selfish, sin-soaked culture. It has been a definite reawakening for me, a challenge to throw off the status quo and to really make a difference in my world. I am convinced that this is a picture of the true church…not a forced sort of family bonding because we all sit in the same building on Sunday, but a true family built out of genuine love for one another. And in those relationships, Christ's love is so evident and so full.

In following the path of radical obedience, I have tasted the mystery of the sacred fellowship that comes when two or more are gathered in His name, and it has added a richness to my life that I would never again want to live without. It is a richness that goes beyond the tradition of the church to a holy existence before a dangerous and untamed God. It is an invitation to live tremblingly joyful before the God of radical obedience and radical grace, the God that I want to know and serve all the days of my life.

Christine has discovered the joy of a heart wholly committed to God. She has discovered that there is no end to what God can do with you—if you let Him.

Where True Change Comes From

How did Christine do it? What changed her walk of faith from ordinary to extraordinary?

Perhaps the better question to ask is *who* changed her walk of faith from ordinary to extraordinary? When we answer that question, we find the true source of radical obedience, and our soul transcends the muck and mire that keeps us from all God has for us.

Radical obedience is not just following a list of right things to do. Nonbelievers can do that and call it "good." Radical obedience is choosing to exchange what is "right" for God's righteousness. Only the pursuit of God's righteousness leads to His best. And it's there we find the source: "God made him who had no sin to be sin for us, so that in him we might become the righteousness of God" (2 Corinthians 5:21).

The answer is simple and complicated all at the same time: It's Jesus. He is our source. He should be the only object of our pursuit. When we accept Jesus Christ as Lord of our life, we exchange our worthless sin for the immeasurable worth of His righteousness.

The apostle Peter put it this way: "But in your hearts set apart Christ as Lord" (1 Peter 3:15). He must be Lord of all if He is our Lord at all. Many people know Christ as their Savior, but the woman who says yes to God longs to know Him as Lord. A person pursuing obedience is able to pause and touch those that He says need our time, in spite of busy schedules. The obedient soul redefines who she is through God's eyes, and any hesitation to do what He asks fades away. This radically obedient woman realizes she is righteous and will find God's best when she pursues right choices that bring glory to Him.

The Love That Compels Us

Yes, becoming women who say yes to God starts with Jesus, and it is His amazing love that compels us:

> For Christ's love compels us, because we are convinced that one died for all, and therefore all died. And he died for all, that those who live should no longer live for themselves but for him who died for them and was raised again. So from now on we regard no one from a worldly point of view. Though we once regarded Christ in this way, we do so no longer. Therefore, if anyone is in Christ, he is a new creation; the old has gone, the new has come! All this is from God, who reconciled us to himself through Christ and gave us the ministry of reconciliation (2 Corinthians 5:14-18).

The love of Christ compels us to choose obedience. Being obedient is not our way of earning God's favor; it is not the path to a more prosperous life. God's favor is with those who love His Son, and our promise of prosperity lies in what we have waiting for us in our eternal home.

Jesus, whose amazing love compels us, said, "If you hold to my teaching, you are really my disciples. Then you will know the truth and the truth will set you free" (John 8:31-32). The truth is the name of Jesus that causes us to pause and redefine ourselves. The truth is the love that compels us to embrace the calling to be Jesus' ambassador. The truth is the freedom to soar above this life and learn to live beyond ourselves and our circumstances.

The real question now becomes do we really want this freedom, this life of ministry that now lies before us? Do we really want to be interrupted in the middle of our busy lives to see God, hear God, and pursue God? Do we really want to be compelled by the love of Christ? Do we really want a Lord of all of our life?

Yes, Jesus, we do.

The Power to Obey

If Christ is the very source of radical obedience, and it is His love that compels us, then it is His power that enables us to do what we're called to do.

Know this: Satan will do everything he can to convince you to say no to God. Satan's very name means "one who separates." He wants to separate you from God's best by offering what seems "very good" from a worldly perspective. He wants you to deny Christ's power in you. He wants to distract you from God's radical purpose for you.

The apostle John warned us of Satan's strategic plan,

Do we really want to be interrupted
in the middle of our busy lives to
see God, hear God, and pursue God?
Do we really want to
be compelled by the love of Christ?
Do we really want a Lord of all of our life?

Do not love the world or anything in the world. If anyone loves the world, the love of the Father is not in him. For everything in the world—the cravings of sinful man, the lust of his eyes and the boasting of what he has and does—comes not from the Father but from the world (1 John 2:15-16).

The *Life Application Bible* offers this insight:

Some people think that worldliness is limited to external behavior—the people we associate with, the places we go, the activities we enjoy. Worldliness is also internal because it begins in the heart and is characterized by three attitudes: 1. the cravings of the sinful man—preoccupation with gratifying physical desires; 2. the lust of his eyes—craving and accumulating things, bowing down to the god of materialism; and 3. boasting of what he has and does—obsession of one's status or importance…By contrast, God values self-control, a spirit of generosity, and a commitment to humble service. It is possible to give the impression of avoiding worldly pleasures while still harboring worldly attitudes in your heart.[1]

It all started way back in paradise with our fruit-loving friend, Eve. She had God's best and traded it all because Satan convinced her that worldly good was more appealing and worth the swap: "When the woman saw that the fruit of the tree was good for food [physical need: the cravings of sinful man] and pleasing to the eye [psychological need: lust of the eyes], and also desirable for gaining wisdom [emotional need: boasting of what he has and does], she took some and ate it [sin separated man from God's best]" (Genesis 3:6). The rest of Genesis 3 covers the shame, hiding, blaming, punishment, and banishment from the Garden.

Well, take heart! This story doesn't end in Genesis 3. Jesus came, and everything changed. He faced temptation just like Eve: "Then

Jesus was led by the Spirit into the desert to be tempted by the devil" (Matthew 4:1). And He was tempted in the same three ways that Eve was tempted, only Jesus' temptations were magnified a hundredfold. Eve was in a lush garden with delicious food, an incredible companion, and all the comforts of paradise. Jesus had been in a desert for 40 days where He went without food, companionship, or comfort of any sort. Satan tempted Him with food that was outside of God's plan for someone who was fasting (physical need: the cravings of sinful man), an opportunity to prove Himself (emotional need: boasting of what he has and does), and the riches of the world (psychological need: lust of the eyes). Jesus withstood the temptations because instead of taking His eyes off of God, He intentionally focused on God and refuted each of Satan's temptations by quoting God's Word.

Satan has no new tricks up his sleeve. He still has nothing better to tempt us with than worldly things. Physical, emotional, and psychological pleasures that fall outside the will of God are still what Satan is using to pull the hearts of God's people away.

For me, the most amazing part of looking at Eve's temptation in relation to Jesus' temptation is what happens next in each of their lives. Eve turns away from God and says yes to worldly distractions. The next chapter of her life is tragic. Eve has two sons, one of whom kills the other. Jesus turns to God and says yes to His divine plan. The next chapter of His life is triumphant. Jesus begins His ministry here on earth. Something will happen next in our life as well. Will the next page in your life be filled with doubts and distractions? Or will it be filled with discovering the blessing of answering God's call on your life?

No Matter What

There are some things God wants us to get settled in our heart. Do we want to chase after the world's emptiness instead of His fullness? Or do we want our lives to be characterized by perfect love instead of perfect performance? Many people halfheartedly claim to be Christians, believing that because we will never be perfect this side of eternity we have an excuse to pursue that which pleases our human longings. Why not push the limits, live for the now, and worry about eternity later? The problem is that we miss the whole point of our existence, the very purpose for which we were created. God made us for the relationship of His perfect love. While we are not capable of perfect performance this side of eternity, we are capable of perfect love. We can settle in our hearts that we will choose God's love and the pursuit of a love relationship with Him above all else, no matter what comes our way.

The day my husband and I made this decision we were in the hospital with our middle daughter, who was six weeks old. She had seemed a perfectly healthy baby until an allergic reaction to the protein in my breast milk landed us in the intensive care unit. The doctors told us on the fourth day of our visit that Ashley needed emergency surgery, and they did not expect her to survive. They gave us five minutes to tell our baby goodbye.

My heart was shattered. I so desperately wanted to scoop her up and run out of the hospital. I wanted to somehow breathe my life into hers. I wanted to take her place. I could handle my own death so much easier than the death of my child. Art prayed over Ashley, we both said our goodbyes, and then with tears streaming down our faces, we let her go.

Art took me outside to the hospital parking lot, where I collapsed into his arms. He gently cupped my face in his hands and reminded me that Ashley was God's child to give and His to take back. "Lysa, God loves Ashley even more than we do," he gently told me. "We must trust His plan."

Art then asked me to do something, and it changed my whole perspective on my relationship with God: "We have to get it settled in our hearts that we will love God no matter the outcome of Ashley's surgery," he said.

At first I resented Art's desire that we love God in this way. I feared it might give Him the impression it was okay to take Ashley. With all my being I wanted to hold on to my child and refuse God. Yet, though I was heartbroken, I also felt God's compassion. I felt Him drawing me close and pouring out His tender mercy. God knew firsthand the pain we were feeling because He'd felt it Himself. I knew that, ultimately, I had no ability to control my child's future. With tears pouring from our eyes, Art and I released our sweet Ashley to the Lord and promised to love Him no matter what.

It was as if the more I fell into God's arms, the less the pain of the moment seared my heart. Feeling the power of God took away the fear of the unknown. I stopped thinking about the what-ifs and let my soul simply say, *Okay. God, in this minute I choose rest with You. I will not let my mind go to the minutes that are coming. I will simply be in this moment and face it with peace.*

That day we settled our love for God not just for this situation but for all time. Though we did not feel at all happy, a gentle covering of unexplainable joy settled over our hearts. Knowing that the One who loved Ashley even more than we did was taking care of her, and that His plan for her was perfect, brought peace in the middle of heartbreak.

The end of this chapter of Ashley's life was miraculous and wonderful. Though the doctors can't explain how, she made a full recovery. Who can understand why God answers prayer the way He does? We just know we're grateful. And we can also know that no matter God's answer, our hearts were settled to trust and love Him. This kind of radical obedience brings about a depth of relationship with God you can't get any other way.

Nothing in life is certain. Circumstances roll in and out like the ocean's tide. The unknown can sometimes seem so frightening as we ponder all the tragic possibilities that we know can and do happen to people. We catch ourselves wondering what the next page of life might hold. We can't stop or control the things that roll our way any more than we can stop the water's edge. But we can make the minute by minute choice to let our souls rest in God.

"Rest knowing all is so safe in My Hands. Rest is Trust. Ceaseless activity is distrust. Without the knowledge that I am working for you, you do not rest. Inaction then would be the outcome of despair. My Hand is not shortened that it cannot save. Know that, repeat it, rely on it, welcome the knowledge, delight in it. Such a truth is as a hope flung to a drowning man. Every repetition of it is one pull nearer shore and safety."[2]

Here Is a Woman Who Gets It!

Recently, I was introduced to a blog written by a woman named Beverly. She is a homeschooling mother battling cancer. As I read the writings of this courageous woman, I couldn't help but say to myself, "Here is a woman who gets it!"

She is a woman fighting for her very life who refuses to get swept up in the bitterness and anxiety that surely come knocking on the door of her heart. She has made the choice to say yes to God every day, in big ways and small. Some of the writings on her blog addressed her cancer. But, surprising to me, most did not. I found her blog entries to be full of her adventures with God. I think what I liked most about the following entry is that it does not wrap up with a sweet little, "Of course, God gave us all the answers and everything turned out just right." She simply found purpose and peace in her choice to experience God.

The parking lot of a Kentucky Fried Chicken. Not exactly where we were planning to spend the first night of our vacation. The day had actually been great. We had spent time at the pool that morning, gone to Wal-Mart for groceries for the week, and then headed down to Pensacola Beach. The beach was wonderful. White sand, beautiful water that was not too robust for my boys, and fairly mild temperatures, considering that it was Florida in July. As we were pulling out of the beach parking lot, our van had stalled. It took Greg a couple of tries to get it going again, but it drove just fine all the way up to the KFC. As I went into the restaurant to get our supper, I called out to Greg not to turn off the engine, just in case there was something wrong. When I returned with our food, the van was not running. It had died when he had parked, and it would not start again. Thus began our two-and-a-half-hour wait. It was already 8:30, and no one had eaten since lunch.

Now, my wonderful husband is very mechanically minded, and he was sure that he could get it going. Of all things, there was an Auto Zone right next door, and he went in to get something. It didn't work. He then wondered if our gasoline gauge had gone bad and we were out of fuel. So back to the Auto Zone for a can and down the road to a station. That wasn't it. At some point I handed out the biscuits from our dinner, since some of the gang were starting to get cranky. Finally, we accepted a ride back to our motel with one of the employees (in shifts, of course, as we would not all fit in her car). We sat down to our chicken dinner at 11:30 PM, and I have to admit that it had rather lost its appeal by then.

The next day we were able to arrange for a mechanic to take Greg over there to look at it, and he agreed with Greg that it was the fuel pump. He had the van towed to his shop, and we stayed in our room and prayed. How much was this going to cost? Would he be able to fix it? What were we going to do without a vehicle? But we also consoled ourselves. God must have a plan. We fantasized over what it might be. Maybe He wanted us to share Christ with the mechanic, and he would give his heart to the Lord. Maybe we would see God's provision by the mechanic fixing the van for free. We just knew that there would be some obvious sign that this was all in God's plan. In the meantime, our boys were well content at the motel with the pool and cable TV, and we had plenty of food.

Two days later our van was fixed. To our knowledge, the mechanic did not accept the Lord. He charged us full price for the work he did, and he wanted cash at that. In other words, we did not see that the Lord had done anything through our trial with our van. We were poorer, but not wiser. Why, Lord, did You allow this to happen?

It would surely be wonderful if life was so prettily packaged, wouldn't it? Every time we had trouble in our life, we could then see the good that came out of it. Oh, for sure, there are plenty of times where we clearly see the hand of God in difficult circumstances. We look back and marvel at how God brought great things out of challenging situations. But there are plenty of times when God, in His own sovereignty, does not open our eyes to what He is doing. He wants us to trust Him, no matter what is happening.

So what does the Bible say about this? Does it guarantee that we will always see what God is doing? The clear answer is no, it doesn't. We walk by faith, not by sight. Hebrews 11 is often called the hall of fame of faith. It outlines the lives of many who went before us, who stood on God's Word despite incredible odds. Verses 39 and 40 say these words, "These were all commended for their faith, yet none of them received what had been promised. God had planned something better for us so that only together with us would they be made perfect." These people all lived waiting for a Savior. Yet they never saw Him in their lifetimes. But they believed. And we too need to believe, even if we don't always see what God is doing.

One day God may open up our spiritual eyes to see what He was doing during our trial with our van. Maybe He just wanted us to learn to be content despite the circumstances. Maybe He wanted us to know how others feel who are experiencing the same thing we did. Maybe we just need to realize that we are living in a fallen world, and vans break down in a fallen world. I don't know. But I do know that God is God, and that I can trust Him no matter what happens in this world.[3]

As I read about Beverly's experience, I thought about how hard it is to stay godly when things in life go awry. Her story caused me to think about the way I might have reacted in her shoes. Her experience wasn't life threatening, but it was life interrupted. For me, sometimes, it is so much harder to pass the small tests of life than the big ones.

I can picture myself thinking, *This was supposed to be a vacation where we take a break from life being hard and unfair. The van can't break now!* Our flesh pulls at our soul to yell and scream and demand things go the way we planned. We don't want inconvenience. We don't want to be tested. We're not even in the mood to be a witness to the participants in our unexpected drama. We want to get in our van, drive back to the motel, eat our dinner, put the kids to bed, and sit out on the balcony in quiet reflection lulled by the sights and sounds of the ocean. But we have a great enemy to the peace we crave, one who loves to interrupt our lives at the most unsuspecting times. Satan wants to catch us off guard and use our reactions against us. He loves to whisper, "If you can't stay godly and obedient in the small mishaps of life, how do you think you're going to be able to pass the bigger tests and trials?" So, in the quietness of our hearts we ponder our reactions to life's situations. And if we find our attitude wanting, we label ourselves unable.

I don't qualify to be a woman who says yes to God. Look at how I acted: impatient, unkind, emotional, angry, unstable, and irrational.

We label ourselves, close up this book, and put it in the tall stack of other unfinished books. I know because I did this for too long in my life. It wasn't until I settled God's amazing love in my heart that I finally understood what Lamentations 3 refers to when it tells us, "His compassions are new every morning." Actually, God's compassions, or mercies, are available minute-by-minute, step-by-step, decision-by-decision, reaction-by-reaction. We don't have to get bogged down and label ourselves as unable. We just have to ask God for forgiveness and move on.

I am not a woman who should be labeled unable. I am a woman on a journey of learning how to make sure my reactions don't deny Christ's presence in me. I am a woman who says yes to God not because my emotions and reactions are always perfect. No, I say yes to God because He is perfectly able to forgive me, love me, remind me, challenge me, and show me how to weather trials in ways that prove His Spirit resides in me. I remind myself often that people don't care to meet my Jesus until they meet the reality of Jesus in my life.

Job was a man who lived this way. He was tested and tried in ways most of us can't imagine. He experienced everything he ever feared: "If only my anguish could be weighed and all my misery be placed on the scales! It would surely outweigh the sand of the seas" (Job 6:2). Even Job's wife said to him, "Are you still holding on to your integrity? Curse God and die!" (Job 2:9). But Job had settled in his heart to trust God: "You are talking like a foolish woman," he told his wife. "Shall we accept good from God, and not trouble?" (Job 2:10). And because of that radical obedience, Job received a radical blessing in his relationship with the Lord: "My ears had heard of you but now my eyes have seen you" (Job 42:5). Job had known of God, but only through his trials and his obedience did he experience God personally.

The psalmist David discovered this radical blessing—this intimate, deep relationship with God—when he settled in his heart to love God no matter what.

> My life is consumed by anguish and my years by groaning; my strength fails because of my affliction, and my bones grow weak...But I trust in you, O Lord; I say, "You are my God." My times are in your hands; deliver me from my enemies and from those who pursue me. Let your face shine on your servant; save me in your unfailing love...How great is your goodness, which you have stored up for those who fear you, which you bestow in the sight of men on those who take refuge in you...Praise be to the Lord, for he showed his wonderful love to me (Psalm 31:10,14-16,19,21).

With God's amazing love settled in our heart, we have His power to keep our faith steady and to experience lasting hope and joy independent of our situation.

It's true—God wants it all. And it's in the exchange of what we want for what God wants that we experience the adventure and freedom and power of saying yes to God.

God is using all of your experiences, both good and bad, to develop your character to match your calling.

After all, dear friend, you *never* know how God will use you until you let Him.

Bible Study

Read 1 Peter 3:15 and record it here.

How are we to set apart Christ?

What does it mean for Him to be Lord?

Lord over what in our lives?

Read Jeremiah 12:2. Describe the person being referred to in this verse.

Where are we to set apart Christ?

Read Jeremiah 11:7-8. What does it mean to have a stubborn heart?

Read Proverbs 13:25 and write the word that describes the condition of the heart of those who live to make right choices that honor God.

Read Psalm 84. Look at verses 1-2 and verse 10:

> How lovely is your dwelling place, O LORD Almighty! My soul yearns, even faints, for the courts of the LORD; my heart and my flesh cry out for the living God…Better is one day in your courts than a thousand elsewhere; I would rather be a doorkeeper in the house of my God than dwell in the tents of the wicked.

This is a person who has decided to chase not after the world's emptiness, but rather God's fullness. The more you are satisfied with God, the more you crave to spend time with Him. Have you ever felt as though your time with the Lord is empty and simply done as another thing to check off your never-ending chore list?

Write a prayer asking God to make your time with Him more meaningful. Ask God to give you a deep desire for Him.

Read Psalm 84:4. What is a common characteristic for those abiding with the Lord?

Is it a common practice for you to praise the Lord? How could you incorporate more praise in your everyday relationship with God?

According to verse 5, where do we draw our strength from? Where should our hearts be set? What type of pilgrimage are we on?

Comment on the following statement from this chapter:

> I am a woman on a journey of learning how to make sure my reactions don't deny Christ's presence in me. I am a woman who says yes to God not because my emotions and reactions are always perfect. No, I say yes to God because He is perfectly able to forgive me, love me, remind me, challenge me, and show me how to weather trials in ways that prove His Spirit resides in me. I remind myself often that people don't care to meet my Jesus until they meet the reality of Jesus in my life.

How does this speak to you, challenge you, and/or encourage you?

How does Psalm 84:9,11 encourage you?

What is surely in store for a woman who says yes to God?

5

What Keeps Us from Saying Yes to God

Whatever we worship, we will obey.

I COULD SEE IT IN THE CROSS expression on her face and in the urgency in her stride. The woman approaching me had a few things on her mind.

Sure enough, this woman in my Bible study class thought I was taking my faith a little too seriously and the Bible a little too literally. After she dumped her load of concern on me, she smiled and encouraged me to lighten up. "Honey," she said, "I wouldn't want to see you carry this obedience thing too far."

This, my friend, is a naysayer. If you choose the life of radical obedience, you are going to encounter such people. They don't understand you. They don't want to understand you. And often what you're doing makes them feel convicted. If someone is quick to find fault in something good someone else is doing, that person is usually wrapped up in his or her own self-centered outlook. Naysayers make themselves feel better by tearing others down. Paul warned Timothy about people like this:

> Mark this: There will be terrible times in the last days. People will be lovers of themselves, lovers of money, boastful, proud, abusive, disobedient to their parents, ungrateful, unholy, without love, unforgiving, slanderous, without self-control, brutal, not lovers of good, treacherous, rash, conceited, lovers of pleasure rather than lovers of God—having a form of godliness but denying its power. Have nothing to do with them (2 Timothy 3:1).

Becoming a woman who unashamedly says yes to God is going to cause you to be different from many of your family members and friends. You will examine life's circumstances with a different outlook. You will perceive things with a different expectation. You will understand that just because life is busy doesn't mean you have to rush about without God. You understand your responsibility is to obey God and He will handle the outcome. When you start to fret or worry, you know how to get swept into God's assurance rather than swept away in fear. You will rely on a strength and power that simply does not make sense to most people.

While not all of your friends and family will be naysayers, some will. The difference naysayers see in you compels them to come against you full force because Christ working through you will sometimes step on the toes of their consciences. While naysayers may talk a good Christian game, they deny Christ in their attitudes and actions toward others. Instead of allowing those feelings of conviction to produce good changes in them, they seek to discourage you in hopes of hushing Christ in you.

It's not easy to keep their negativity from being discouraging, but as my husband always reminds me, "Lysa, consider the source." I ask myself, "Is this person criticizing me active in pursuing a relationship with the Lord? Is this person answering God's call on his life, producing the evidence of Christ's fruit? Does he have my best interest in mind?" The answers are almost always no. So I look for any truth that might be in what this person has said, forgive him for any hurt he may have caused, and let the rest go.

What about when the person causing the hurt and becoming a source of discouragement is a strong believer? Even strong believers pursuing God can get pulled into ungodly attitudes. If only people had flashing signs above their heads that gave warning when they were operating in the flesh instead of the Spirit. A wise friend once gave me a real nugget of truth that I think about often. She warned me as I stepped out and determined to say yes to God in all things, "Never let others' compliments go to your head or their criticisms go to your heart."

Author Rick Warren, in his book *The Purpose-Driven Life*, comments on naysayers:

> You will find that people who do not understand your shape for ministry will criticize you and try to get you to conform to what they think you should be doing. Ignore them. Paul often had to deal with critics who misunderstood and maligned his service. His response was always the same: Avoid comparisons, resist exaggerations, and seek only God's commendation.[1]

Rick then goes on to quote John Bunyan as saying, "If my life is fruitless, it doesn't matter who praises me, and if my life is fruitful, it doesn't matter who criticizes me."

That's so true!

But I know firsthand how hard it is to live in that truth.

The Foes of Grace

Grace for the journey...we all need it. God is the only one we should be living for, and we need His grace to handle the successes and the failures, the applause and the criticism, and everything in-between. Sometimes our efforts will be fruitful and other times fruitless. But as long as we please God, it's all for good.

Grace has two fierce foes, though—acceptance and rejection. Imagine, for a moment, a tall, gated wall. Puddles of mud dot the well-worn, barren ground. It is evident that many have lingered here. Two gatekeepers wish to detain you. They wish to take your hand in friendship and have you remain on the outside of the wall. All the while, Jesus is standing on the other side of the wall in an open field full of beauty and adventure. So few have actually made it past the gatekeepers into this field that the blades of grass remain unbroken and the flowers unpicked.

The first gatekeeper is Acceptance. He requires much of me. He seems so enticing with his offerings of compliments and big promises. But though he is fun for a moment, soon my mind is flooded with concerns of being able to continue to impress him. I am quickly over-whelmed with pondering my interactions with others and keeping score on the table of comparison.

The second gatekeeper is Rejection. He also requires much of me. He seems appealing because he gives me permission to excuse myself from following my true calling. Yet he demands that I pull back and shy away from the obedience for which my soul longs. His whispered questions of "What if?" and "What do they think of you?" linger in my mind and influence my actions and reactions.

How do I deny the lure of these two gatekeepers of grace? After all, I've tasted their laced fruit and, though I'm aware of their poison, I also crave their sweetness. In my flesh I desire the praises of Acceptance and the excuses of Rejection. The limelight of Acceptance shines on the pride that has yet to be driven from my heart. The thought that I am really something denies the reality that, but for the grace of Christ, I am nothing. The ease of settling for less is the pull of Rejection. When I listen to him, I shrink back and pull inside myself. I no longer want to press on. I want to quit. The thought that I am really nothing eclipses the reality that, because of the grace of Christ in me, I am a treasured something.

So goes the battle in my heart. Honestly, it sickens me that I even give thought to and feel enticed by these life-draining agents of Satan. Jesus is standing behind these two slick gatekeepers. His arms are open, waiting to embrace and enfold me in the security of His truth. His truth is that I am precious and accepted, no matter what. No matter what choices I make, His love is not based on my performance. His love is based on His perfect surrender at the cross. But, I must choose to accept this love and walk this truth for it to make a difference in how I journey through life.

The Great Dance

Pursuing obedience and saying yes to God has been the most fulfilling adventure I have ever let my heart follow after. However, the journey has not been without bumps and bruises. I would be remiss in this chapter of what keeps us from radical obedience if I did not talk about the great dance between the desire of our flesh and the desire of God's Spirit in us. Our flesh seeks the approval of others, is swayed by Satan's voice of condemnation, and looks for the comfortable way out. God's Spirit in us opposes Satan and the world's way and offers an unexplainable peace that transcends the circumstances around us.

The dance plays out in rather subtle voices in my head. There is the pull between condemnation and conviction. If I'm hearing thoughts of condemnation, these only come from Satan. There is no condemnation from Jesus, only conviction. It's important for us to know the difference. Condemnation leaves us feeling hopeless and worthless. Conviction invites us to make positive changes in our lives.

I also sometimes find myself getting caught up in my own weariness and grumbling over the empty places of my life. These are all the places

No matter what choices I make,
His love is not based on my performance.
His love is based on
His perfect surrender at the cross.

that chip away at my contentment, that nag me into thinking I'm being cheated out of something somehow. Last year we did a renovation on the house. Things were new and perfect for a couple of days. But it didn't take long with five kids and a dog for the carpet to get stained and the woodwork to get scratched. My car has dings on each of the front doors and a scratch on the driver's side door, and sometimes this bothers me. We won't even talk about what the inside of my kid-toting vehicle looks like! With all of their great qualities, my kids sometimes pout, complain, and whine, and, you guessed it, this bothers me. My husband and I are crazy about each other but still find ways to get on each other's nerves at times, and this bothers me. I struggle with trying to cram too much into too little time and often find myself running late—which really bothers me. When these little things get piled on top of bigger things, I can really get down.

There are things in my life, little and big, that fall short, don't meet my expectations, and cause grumpy feelings inside my heart. Do you ever sense empty places in your life too?

Usually this happens to me when the busyness of life has crowded out my quiet times with Jesus. When I have not spent enough time allowing the Lord to refuel and refill me, I forget that this is not my real home. When my soul gets down, these places can be distracting and difficult. And sometimes the reality is we feel hurt and discouraged.

The Choice to Worry or Worship

When we find ourselves in these hard places, we make the choice to worry or worship. When we worry, we feel we have to come up with justifications and careful explanations for the naysayers. When we worry, we listen to the voices of Acceptance and Rejection. When we worry, we lay awake at night and ponder Satan's lies. When we worry, we have pity parties where the guests of honor are Negative Thinking, Doubt, and Resignation.

But we can make the choice to worship. When we worship in these hard places, we are reminded that none of this is about us—it's all about God. We turn our focus off of ourselves and back onto God Almighty. God can use empty places in your life to draw your heart to Him. He is the great love of your life who will never disappoint. He is building your eternal home that will never get broken, dirty, or need redecorating. He is preparing a place of eternal perfect fellowship where no one will be a naysayer. And heaven won't be limited to human time frames, so no one will ever be late...not even me!

Our hearts were made for perfection in the Garden of Eden, but the minute sin came into the picture, strokes of imperfection began to cast a dingy hue. When we know Christ, however, we know this is not all there is. Realizing that this life is temporary helps me to live beyond this moment and rejoice in what is to come. Each time I feel my heart being pulled down into the pit of ungratefulness and grumbling, I recognize it as a call to draw near to the Lord. I thank Him for the empty places, for they remind me that only He has the ability to fill me completely. In my worship of Him, my soul is safe and comforted and reassured and at peace.

We all worship something. We must choose whom—or what—we will worship. Will it be the opinions of others, our fears, or even our own comfort? Or will it be the One who created our souls to worship? Whatever we worship, we will obey. As we choose to be radically obedient and say yes to the Lord, we must be radical about choosing to worship Him and Him alone.

Peace like a River

What is the result of choosing to worship God, to obey Him alone? "Peace is the fruit of the obedient, righteous life."[2] If I am ever going to find peace past the naysayers, past the attacks of Satan, and past my own weariness, it will only be because I choose daily to walk in absolute

We must choose whom—or what—
we will worship.
Will it be the opinions of others,
our fears, or even our own comfort?
Or will it be the One who
created our souls to worship?
Whatever we worship, we will obey.

obedience to the moment-by-moment, day-by-day, assignment-by-assignment commands of the Lord.

The prophet Isaiah writes, "If only you had paid attention to my commands, your peace would have been like a river, your righteousness like the waves of the sea" (Isaiah 48:18). Did you catch the treasure hidden here? One of the most radical blessings for the woman saying yes to God is the peace that rushes through the soul of the one who is attentive to the Lord's commands.

God chose such a unique word to describe His peace—a river! A river is not calm and void of activity. It is active and cleansing and confident of the direction it is headed in. It doesn't get caught up with the rocks in its path. It flows over and around them, all the while smoothing their jagged edges and allowing them to add to its beauty rather than take away from it. A river is a wonderful thing to behold. Beth Moore says, "To have peace like a river is to have security and tranquility while meeting the many bumps and unexpected turns on life's journey. Peace is submission to a trustworthy Authority, not resignation from activity."[3]

Jesus tells us His peace is unlike the world's peace: "Peace I leave with you; my peace I give you. I do not give to you as the world gives. Do not let your hearts be troubled and do not be afraid" (John 14:27). The world's way to peace would have me pull back to make life a little easier for me, my circumstances, and my family. The problem with this is that we were not put here to be all about ourselves—we were put here to be all about God. We are to die to our self-centeredness so we can have more of Christ in our hearts and minds. Jesus clearly tells us to focus on Him, His ways, and His example, and His peace will be with us. The focus of our hearts and minds will shape our decisions and actions that follow: "You [God] will keep in perfect peace him whose mind is steadfast, because he trusts in you" (Isaiah 26:3).

When we focus our minds and fix our attention on Christ, He is magnified and made bigger in our lives. When we focus our minds and fix our attention on life's obstacles, they will be wrongly magnified and made to appear larger than they really are. Our attention is like a magnifying glass—whatever we place it on becomes larger and more consuming of our time and energy. We desire to focus on Christ alone, but sometimes other things seem bigger, and so, without even realizing it, we shift our focus: "For the sinful nature desires what is contrary to the Spirit, and the Spirit what is contrary to the sinful nature. They are in conflict with each other, so that you do not do what you want" (Galatians 5:17). Before we know it, we are drawn into the muck and mire on the outer banks of Jesus' river of peace.

But sometimes it is down on your face in the mud in complete humility (and sometimes even humiliation!) that you will find a sweet and tender truth. It's from this position that you can say, "Jesus, I love You and want You more than anything else. I love You and want You more than the approval of my peers, family and friends, and even the naysayers in my life. I love You and want You more than the comforts and trappings of this world. I love You and choose to believe Your truth over Satan's lies. I love You and choose to worship You and You alone. Jesus, I love You and want to come to You empty-handed and offer my life in complete surrender."

Saying yes to God is a lot more about being than doing. It is choosing who I will worship and then depending on God to give me the strength to follow through. As my soul looks up from life's muck and rights the focus of its attention, I find myself pressing back into the river, where Jesus' peace rushes over me, refreshing, cleansing, and invigorating.

A Little Girl's Dance

My touch has always comforted my youngest daughter, Brooke. I can remember running errands when she was a baby, knowing we should have been home an hour earlier for her nap. But also knowing there were things that had to get done, I pressed on, hoping for the best. She started getting fussy, which made everyone else in the car start to lose patience. One of my older daughters, feeling very wise at five years old, said, "Mom, just tell her to stop crying. Tell her she'll get in big trouble if she doesn't."

Well, that might make a toddler who wouldn't want to miss out on watching *Barney* that afternoon settle down, but it did not work with a baby. She wanted to get out of that car and she wanted to make sure we all knew it. What started as some whines and whimpers soon escalated into a full-blown meltdown complete with tears, wailing, and screaming.

I couldn't do much to comfort her while trying to drive, but I could reach my arm into the backseat and gently pat her leg. It took a few minutes, but eventually she settled down and reached her tiny hand out to hold mine.

All of my kids like a hug, a pat on the shoulder, a hand of comfort on their back, but to Brooke these gentle touches seem to be a lifeline. Maybe touch is her love language. As Gary Chapman puts it in his book *The Five Love Languages,* touch might be the way Brooke will speak and understand love the most. Whatever it is, my touch is important to Brooke.

Recently, she had a performance with her praise dance team from school. All the girls looked especially beautiful that day dressed all in white, their hair pulled gently back from their faces, and each had an extra measure of grace in their step. I couldn't wait to see Brooke perform these dances she'd been working on and talking about for weeks. She loves getting up on a stage, so I expected her to be full of smiles and giggles. But just a few minutes before the performance was about to begin a very distraught Brooke made her way to the audience to find me. With tears streaming down her cheeks, she explained that the teacher had moved her from the front row to the back row, and she didn't know the back row's part. I assured her everything would be fine.

I whispered, "Honey, just get up there and watch the other girls for cues and follow in step. You know this dance, Brooke. You'll be fine."

She sobbed back, "I won't be fine if I mess up, and I know I'm going to mess up."

That's when it occurred to me. She would need my touch to get through this. But she and I both knew that it would not be possible for my arm to reach all the way up to the stage. So I quickly whispered, "Brooke, lock your eyes with mine, and Mommy will touch you with my smile. Don't look at anyone or anything else. Don't even look at the other girls dancing. It doesn't matter if you mess up. What matters is that you keep your eyes on me the whole time. We'll do this together."

Quietly she asked, "The whole time, Mommy?"

"The whole time, Brooke," I replied as I watched my brave girl walk away to take her place in line.

Several times during the dance, Brooke fell out of step. Her arms would go down when the rest of the back row lifted theirs up. She would go left and bump into the others headed right. She knew her steps weren't perfect, so her eyes brimmed with tears. However, the tears never fell. With her eyes perfectly locked on my smiling face, she danced. She danced when the steps came easy. She danced when her steps got jumbled. She danced even when her emotions begged her to quit. She danced the whole way through. She danced and I smiled.

I smiled when her steps were right on track. I smiled when they weren't. My smile was not based on her performance. My smile was born out of an incredible love for this precious, courageous little girl. As she kept her attention focused solely on my smile and the touch of my gaze, it was as if the world slowly faded away and we were the only ones in the room.

This is the way God wants me to dance through life.

Though I can't physically see Him, my soul pictures Him so clearly. In my mind's eye He is there. The touch of His gaze wraps about me, comforts me, assures me, and makes the world seem strangely dim. As long as my gaze is locked on His, I dance and He smiles. The snickers and jeers of others fade away. Though I hear their razor sharp intentions, they are unable to pierce my heart and distract my focus. Even my own stumblings don't cause the same feelings of defeat. My steps so often betray the desire of my heart, but it is not my perfect performance that captures His attention. Rather, it is my complete dependence on Him that He notices.

He then whispers, "Hold on to Me and what I say about you. For My words are the truth of who you are and the essence of what you were created to be." I then imagine Him pausing and, with tears in His eyes and a crack in His voice, He adds, "Then you will know the truth, and the truth will set you free" (John 8:32).

His truth frees you from the chains of doubt and despair. His truth frees me from feeling unable and inadequate to try and pursue God in an all-out way. His truth washes over me as I tentatively whisper, "I want to be a woman who says yes to God." And in that moment, with my eyes locked on His, I am.

Bible Study

When faced with the choice to worry or to worship, which Scripture will be a powerful reminder for you of God's certain help?

Read Matthew 6:26-27. What good will worry do?

Read Matthew 6:30-32. What does God promise for our provision?

Read Matthew 6:34. How can we let go of worries for the future?

Read Mark 13:10-11. While you might not get arrested for preaching the gospel, you may find yourself in a situation where you are worried how to speak. How does this comfort you?

Instead of worrying, the mark of our life should be worship. Worship replaces anxiety brought on by fear with an unexplained peace that can only come from focusing on God.

> My *eyes* are *fixed* on you, O Sovereign LORD; in you I take refuge—do not give me over to death (Psalm 141:8, emphasis added).

Remember the story I shared about Brooke fixing her eyes on me when she faced fear? What does fixed in this verse mean? What does taking refuge in the Lord mean? How can we fix our eyes on the Lord?

Read Isaiah 30:21.

What voice is being referred to here?

What direction will this voice give us?

How does this calm your worries?

> Let us fix our eyes on Jesus, the *author* and *perfecter* of our
> faith, who for the joy set before him endured the cross, scorning
> its shame, and sat down at the right hand of the throne of God
> (Hebrews 12:2, emphasis added).

What does it mean that Jesus is the author of our faith? What does it mean that Jesus is the perfecter of our faith? How does this verse comfort and encourage you?

Most people assume that Saint Patrick is from Ireland. This is not true. St. Patrick was actually kidnapped as a teen from his native land of Britain and forced to be a slave for six years in Ireland. During his captivity, his job was tending sheep. He spent many hours each day in prayer. By the time he escaped back to Britain, he was no longer a self-centered aristocratic child. He had become a man sold out for the cause of Christ. Several years later, he returned as a missionary to Ireland and lived out his life winning that country to Christ.

His life circumstances often could have caused a lot of worry. Instead, he made the choice to worship God and trust His plan. I thought his constant prayer would inspire you:

Christ shield me this day:
Christ with me,
Christ before me,
Christ behind me,
Christ in me,
Christ beneath me,
Christ above me,

Christ on my right,
Christ on my left,
Christ when I lie down,
Christ when I arise,
Christ in the heart of every person who thinks of me,
Christ in every eye that sees me,
Christ in the ear that hears me.

SAINT PATRICK,
FROM HIS BREASTPLATE

6

If It Were Easy, It Wouldn't Be Worth Doing

Radical obedience is born out of delight, not duty.

I WAS DISCOURAGED. IN two months' time my life went from being wonderfully fulfilling and clicking right along to completely topsy-turvy. I felt myself getting caught in a whirlwind of emotions. My computer went on the blink and some very important documents disappeared. A big book deal I was excited about fell through. Our well broke, and we had to go several days without water. A diamond fell out of my wedding ring.

Then, on top of a host of other interruptions and haphazard happenings, my husband blew out his knee and had to have major reconstructive surgery, leaving him bedridden for nearly five weeks. I didn't know whether to laugh or cry. A friend of mine hit the nail on the head when she said, "Lysa, I think when you go with God to a new level, you get a new devil."

While I'm not sure about the exact theological correctness of that

If our desire for obedience is
born merely out of duty,
we may be quick to give up.
However, if our desire is born out of delight,
out of a love relationship
that burns deep in our soul,
it won't be extinguished—no matter the cost.

statement, I do know that Satan hates the radically obedient soul. He hates it when a person jumps off the fence of complacency and into the center of God's will. There is a spiritual battle raging around us and, because of that, life can be hard. While saying yes to God does bring blessing, it's not easy. If our desire for obedience is born merely out of duty, we may be quick to give up. However, if our desire is born out of delight, out of a love relationship that burns deep in our soul, it won't be extinguished—no matter the cost.

Purpose, Perspective, Persistence

One of my favorite love stories in the Bible is that of Jacob and Rachel. Jacob's love for Rachel gave him purpose and perspective which led to amazing persistence. He served Rachel's father for many years to earn the right to marry Rachel because he loved her that much: "So Jacob served seven years to get Rachel, but they seemed like only a few days to him because of his love for her" (Genesis 29:20).

Do you see what love can do for a person's view of his circumstances? When you are crazy in love with someone, you'll do anything for him—and do it with the highest level of sheer joy. I want to be so crazy in love with Jesus that not only do I serve Him, but I do it with absolute delight.

A real sign of spiritual maturity is looking to God not for comfort and convenience but for purpose and perspective. Comfort and convenience lead to complacency. When trouble comes, the complacent person becomes critical of everyone, including God. On the other hand, purpose and perspective lead to the perseverance that is evident in those living a truly devoted life. The persistent person eagerly looks to handle trials and struggles in a way that honors God and allows personal growth.

Because we love God, we look for and trust in His purpose in everything. The persistent person understands the meaning of Romans 8:28:

A real sign of spiritual maturity
is looking to God
not for comfort and convenience
but for purpose and perspective.

"We know that in all things God works for the good of those who love him, who have been called according to his purpose." This does not mean that everything that happens to us will be good, but that God will work in and through every situation to bring good from it. And let's not miss the last four words of this verse, where we are reminded that it is all "according to His purpose." God has a purpose, and His plans to accomplish that purpose are perfect. Trusting God's good purpose, and seeking to understand that He takes all the events from our life and orchestrates good from them, leads to a changed perspective.

Seeing God in Everything

Our changed perspective helps us see God in everything. I am convinced that Satan wants to keep my perspective in a place where my heart is discouraged and my mind is questioning God. Yet God's Word calls me to a different action: "We also rejoice in our sufferings, because we know that suffering produces perseverance; perseverance, character; and character, hope" (Romans 5:3). God's Word calls me to rejoice! Not that I rejoice in the bad things—I would have to fake that. But I *can* rejoice in what God is doing in me through difficult times.

When Art hurt his knee, we prayed and prayed this would be a minor injury and surgery wouldn't be required. We just knew God was going to go before us and make the way smooth for this injury. However, when the test results came back, we were facing a worst-case scenario. Not only would Art have to have surgery, but it was one of the worst knee injuries the doctor had ever seen. Simply looking at the circumstances and the doctor's report, we might have been tempted to get pulled into Satan's lies that God had not answered our prayers, that He wasn't trustworthy. However, the truth is that God is faithful and true, and His Word promises us, "He has not despised or disdained the suffering of the afflicted one; he has not hidden his face from him but listened to his cry for help" (Psalm 22:24).

So what do we do with the fact that my very athletic husband is out of commission for several months? What does he do about missing many weeks of work and having his life totally interrupted? What do I do with my feelings of being overwhelmed and frustrated because I need his help with the kids? What do I do with the fact that he can't drive, is in extreme pain, and needs my unconditional love and support—even on the days when I'm too tired to give it?

Okay, God, where are You? I cried out. There were too many details and too much stress. Our everyday life was already too busy, and now this. To be completely honest, I started to get a little frustrated with God. Satan was having a field day.

Provision, Protection, Process

What do you do when you feel as though God isn't hearing your cries for help? Or, worse yet, He's saying no?

It hasn't been easy, and God has had to remind me several times, but here's what I do know: God *always* hears me when I cry out to Him, and when He says no, it's for my provision, my protection, and it's part of the process of growing me more like Christ.

Provision

On one of my "Woe is me, my husband is still in bed and I am still doing everything" days, I took my kids along with a friend's child out to lunch. I was determined to have a good attitude, but with each whiney response and sibling spat I could feel my blood pressure rising. I was at the counter trying to place my order and keep an eye on the kids sitting in the booth across the restaurant when a lady came up and put her hand gently on my shoulder. "I've got your napkins and straws," she said, "and I'll put them on your table." I was shocked. Who was this sweet stranger?

After I made my way back to my table, I found her sitting with her family and went over to thank her. When I did, she told me that when I walked into the restaurant, God told her to help me. She didn't know who I was until I turned around to talk to her at the counter, and she recognized me as the speaker from a women's conference she attended last spring. She then went on to ask me if she could make my family a meal. I told her that my husband had just had surgery and a meal would be great.

I walked back to my booth with tears in my eyes. Just that morning I had cried out to God to fill in the gaps where I was feeling weary and weak. I asked Him to be my portion of all I needed to take care of my family that day. God was answering my prayer! My perspective totally changed. God was working good from Art's surgery. He had said no to us not having to have surgery, but He didn't leave us in that hard spot. He was teaching us about His provision.

How can He be our Ultimate Provider if we aren't ever lacking and in need? I was so touched by this lady's obedience to God's call to reach out to me. I was blown away by the personal and practical way God answered my cries for help despite my bad attitude.

Protection

My husband is an avid runner and can often be seen running the country roads near our home. After his knee injury occurred, he was very disappointed, to say the least, when the doctor told him it could be up to a year before he could run again—and that some people with this type of injury have to give up running altogether. Anytime we have to take a break from something we really enjoy, it's hard. But the thought of forever giving up running seemed too much to swallow.

Then came the call from a friend who knew of a man who was injured playing flag football the same week that Art had been injured, only the doctors were telling him he would never walk again. He was now paralyzed from the waist down. Then another call came from a friend who told me she read in the paper of a man riding his bike on the same roads my husband runs on. This man was struck by a car and killed.

Art and I had been so quick to throw a pity party over our circumstances, but now we were coming to the realization that God had protected him from situations that could have been a lot worse.

I confess I don't always understand the ways of God in these circumstances—why Art would just need surgery while another man lay paralyzed and another man was killed. Many have had to go through severe circumstances and unfathomable pain, and my own family is no exception. We have experienced tragedy. But I know that I know that I know: God has worked good in every one of these situations. As I look back and reflect on our difficult times, I can see how He has protected us.

Part of the Process

Ultimately, our time here on earth is for one single purpose: to grow more and more like Christ. Each of us comes to a place in our Christian journey where we have to make the decision whether we will become part of that process or not. I wrote a poem to express that moment of decision:

> *A man journeyed to a place*
> *Where the road caused him to ponder,*
> *Should he travel the wide, clear road?*
> *Or should he venture up the other?*
>
> *The wide road was more often traveled,*
> *It was level and easy and clear.*
> *The narrow one seemed barely a path,*
> *With very few footprints there.*

His senses said to choose for ease
And walk where many have wandered.
But the map he held in his hand
Showed the narrow going somewhere grander.

In life we will all come to a point
Where a decision must be made.
Will we choose to walk with comfort's guide?
Or journey the narrow path God says?

We want to live the totally sold-out life for Christ, yet there are other things pulling at us, enticing us, calling out to us—causing our indecision. Brent Curtis and John Eldredge said it well in their book *The Sacred Romance:*

> At some point on our Christian journey, we all stand at the edge of those geographies where our heart has been satisfied by less-wild lovers, whether they be those of competence and order or those of indulgence. If we listen to our heart again, perhaps for the first time in a while, it tells us how weary it is of the familiar and indulgent. We find ourselves once again at the intersection with the road that is the way of the heart. We look down it once more and see what appears to be a looming abyss between the lovers we have known and the mysterious call of Christ.[1]

In times where the road diverges in front of us, we can either fall away from God or fall toward Him. During Art's long healing process, he made the decision to fall toward God and humbly thank Him for allowing the injury to happen. He chose to look for opportunities every day to rejoice in this trial and make the most of being still and quiet. He dove into God's Word and spent hours praying, reading, and writing notes about all God was teaching him.

Christmas happened to fall right in the middle of Art's recovery. Every Christmas morning we have a special breakfast with Jesus where we give Him a gift from our heart. I wondered what gift Art would have this year. When his turn came, he said he wanted to look for a way to serve another or give to another in Christ's name every day for the next year. By next Christmas he will know that 365 people's lives were made better because of Christ in him. Throughout the following months our dinnertime conversations each night centered around what "God adventures" Daddy had participated in that day. Soon, we were all sharing our own ways that we listened to God. My sweet husband made a choice to rejoice in the process of growing more like Christ, and what a difference it made not only in his life, but in others' lives as well.

I've especially seen a difference in my children. It is a good thing to talk about your faith and make going to church a priority, but when your kids participate in adventures with God and see truth lived out in front of their eyes, He becomes too real to deny. What a joy for me to hear my kids talking about God speaking to them to reach out to someone. How it lights my heart up to hear my kids tell us a story of them making a good decision, though the wrong one seemed more appealing. What comfort there is seeing proof that our kids are pursuing their own relationship rather than just buying into the God thing because of family tradition.

My husband's injury and time spent recovering turned out to be a blessing. What we gained as a family during this time was more than a new perspective; it was a gift from God. This time of looking for ways to serve God like never before prepared our hearts for the night we met our boys in August of that year. We were all so in tune with saying yes to God in the little things that when this big thing came, we faced it head-on. We didn't run away with a trail of good excuses flying about behind us like dust on a dirt road. No, we looked at the opportunity before us, asked for God's will to be done, and leapt into the unknown with nothing but God's sweet confirmations.

Has it been completely easy and without challenge? No. We've had days where my husband and I look at each other in a daze and think

How did we get here? How did we get to this place where five (FIVE!) children all need something from us? This place is messy and loud and full of irresponsible choices. This place where things are never where they are supposed to be...the scissors are lost, the remote control misplaced, and the phone sounds garbled and full of static after being dropped in the pool. The same pool that is not clean at this present moment because someone broke the tube that connects the automatic skimmer to the pump.

But this place is also full of life. This place is full of joy. This place is full of five amazing young people whom God fashioned and designed for some glorious purpose. What a privilege it is to be the ones who get to watch what God is doing to draw their hearts to His. Three of my children were born from my womb and two from my heart, but either way, this parenting thing is a beautiful unfolding of an eternal story. Reflecting this thought is a sign that hangs above my bed that reads, "All because two people fell in love." Two people fell in love, not just with each other but also with the God who drew them together.

Look at all that might have been missed had God answered our prayers about Art's knee the way we wanted Him to. We wanted a quick, easy healing where life could carry on. God wanted life interrupted. God wanted our attention. God wanted to give a huge blessing wrapped in a most unlikely package.

The prophet Jeremiah wrote, "Because of the LORD's great love we are not consumed, for his compassions never fail. They are new every morning; great is your faithfulness. I say to myself, 'The Lord is my portion; therefore I will wait for him' " (Lamentations 3:22-24). God is our portion of protection and peace. He's our portion of provision and security. He's our portion of all of the joy and patience we need during the process of growing more like Christ. He is our portion of whatever we need, whenever we need it—if only we'll recall His goodness and ask Him.

It isn't going to be easy. But we have Jesus and His power, and that power is able to completely change our outlook on life. This is how we can find the kind of joy the apostle Peter talks about: "Though you have not seen him, you love him; and even though you do not see him now, you believe in him and are filled with an inexpressible and glorious joy" (1 Peter 1:8). This is a radical blessing for the radically obedient—the ability to have a radically different perspective.

We're human. We know we're not always going to like our circumstances. Just because I am a woman who says yes to God does not mean I always like the things that come my way on any given day. I do not like some of the things my husband does. I sometimes find myself aggravated and annoyed because he processes things differently and looks at the world in a very black-and-white way. Mix this with my emotional views and hormonal responses, and the product is what we affectionately call "growth opportunities." I've faced a lot of things just this week that I don't particularly like. I already mentioned the scissors, remote control, and telephone. In addition, the girls were swinging too roughly on the hammock and it broke. My son burned my favorite pot. Somehow, most of my nice forks are missing. Though we haven't had enough rain lately to keep the grass green, the weeds are thriving. And ants have taken up residence in my kitchen and bathroom. Maybe they are still looking for remnants of a science experiment gone bad, which caused a smell to breed in our home that only creatures born from larvae could be attracted to.

I don't wake up and think, "Joy, joy, joy. I love misplaced and broken things. I love setting my table with stainless steel knives and plastic forks. I love phones with static. I love weeds and ants with messed-up smellers." No, I wake up and say, "God, I love You and choose to accept the assignments You place before me with an attitude that reflects the truth that You live in me. I know I won't do this perfectly, and I admit my inability to do this in my strength. So, I say yes to You today. I say yes to Your desire to invade my natural flesh responses. I say yes to Your forgiveness when I mess up. I say yes to persevering even when I want to give up. I say yes to Your invitation to be obedient even when other paths seem more appealing. I say yes even as my lips desire to utter a thousand times over, 'I can't.' I say yes to loving You more."

No More "I Can'ts"

Yesterday a friend came over to my house and saw a copy of my book *Radically Obedient, Radically Blessed* sitting on a chair. It was obvious from the dog-eared pages and the pen sticking out from the top that I'd been reading and studying my own book. She teased me about this and then admitted that this was one of my books she doubted she'd ever read. "That just screams of impossibilities to me. Radical obedience? No, I can't do that." I explained I wasn't reading my own book as some type of strange ego booster, but rather because my publisher had asked me to expand this small book and add a Bible study. Then it would be re-released under the title *What Happens When Women Say Yes to God.* She did not recant her earlier thoughts about the book. She still had the same look on her face. The look that reflected an attitude that I've been swept away by many times…"I can't."

These two words can seem quite innocent and reflective of some obvious truths. I can't fly through the air like Superman. I can't make my scalp suddenly start growing the silky straight blond hair that the Pantene hair model so beautifully tosses across the pages of a magazine ad. I can't grow a tree in my backyard that sprouts dollar bills. (Oh, but wouldn't it be such fun if I could!) These statements are truths born from cold hard facts and not from my own laziness or fear.

Other "I can't" statements *are* often born from laziness or fear. Assumptions that have been around so long that they feel like truth. Last summer I decided to take an honest assessment of some of these "I can'ts" in my life. As I marched up to each of these giants, I asked myself the question: What would it take to slay this giant in my life?

I say yes to You today. I say yes to Your desire
to invade my natural flesh responses.
I say yes to Your forgiveness when I mess up.
I say yes to persevering even when I want
to give up. I say yes to Your invitation to
be obedient even when other paths seem
more appealing. I say yes even as my
lips desire to utter a thousand times over,
"I can't." I say yes to loving You more.

Most of the time, the answer was as simple as a decision. "Decide that you ought to, you can, and you will."

I shared this sentiment with a friend who was struggling with her own "I can't." She had known God was calling her to be a speaker and a writer and had signed up for a conference our ministry offers every year called She Speaks. Then the doubts and fears started to overwhelm her. She wrote to me saying:

> Dear Lysa,
>
> I am looking forward to the upcoming conference with a great deal of fear and trembling. I feel like somewhat of an idiot putting myself on the writers' track because I have done so little writing since college. I have been afraid to respond to the appointment schedule because I am fearful of looking like a jerk in front of people I hope to impress. Do you have any suggestions for me? I will have a book proposal, but I feel like a third grader who has been asked to submit a high school term paper. I can hardly tell my friends and family where I am going. They will surely wonder, *Why would she be going to a conference like that?* I walk into Christian bookstores, and I am convinced that it has all been covered.
>
> What is my deal? Last fall I knew without a shadow of a doubt that this was what the Lord wanted me to write. Now I feel as though I am chasing a pipe dream. I have a haunting sense I should just give it up and get back to gardening.

I quickly began a response back to her. It read:

> I love your honesty, sweet friend. I also love your heart. Though you are scared, you are walking that narrow road of absolute obedience. God is pleased.
>
> Now to address your questions and fears. First of all, you are not an idiot at all. You have taken a step toward a dream God has placed in your heart. That makes you obedient, not idiotic. I

am so proud of you for doing more than 90 percent of all people who lurk in the shadows of their dreams but never get intentional about them.

Before I could continue I felt that gentle nudging in my heart that I've come to recognize as God's voice. He brought to my mind another conversation I'd had with this friend where she's shared with me about her running several times a week with a group of ladies from her neighborhood. She was getting in such good shape and feeling great. I just smiled and nodded while thinking, *I could never run that far or be that disciplined.*

God brought this past conversation to my mind, I'm convinced, to challenge me. How could I ask her to step out of her comfort zone into a world where I feel very comfortable, that of speaking and writing, if I wasn't willing to do the same? My advice and encouragement would mean so much more to her if I stepped into her comfort zone and pushed through my own fears. It was time to strap on my tennis shoes and run.

Running more than a mile or two was a big "I can't" in my life. But I felt God telling me to go out and run until I couldn't run anymore. Every time my body wanted to stop, I was to pray for my friend. I ran and ran and ran. When I finally stopped, I immediately got in my car and clocked how far I'd gone. I was shocked as the odometer turned to a little more than three miles. I had done it. I threw my hands up in victory and prepared to retire my tennis shoes for eternity.

That is, until a few days later when God nudged my heart again to run. I continued to run several times a week over the next month and prayed for my friend every time my side ached, my breathing became labored, and my legs cried out for me to stop. I pushed through the "I can't." Then, the day before the conference I threw my hands up as I victoriously exclaimed, "I can!" That day I clocked 8.6 miles.

My friend was also victorious that weekend as she attended the conference, met with publishers, and determined to press on with this calling in her life. And you'd better believe that we carved out time early one morning during the conference to run together. In both of our situations there was nothing standing in our way but our own minds repeating the life-draining words that hold too many people back: "I can't."

I can assure you on the other side of every "I can't" excuse is a glorious adventure with God just waiting to happen. And rest assured, the victory is not found in your performance. Rather, it's in your pursuit of taking that first step with God. A joy will be there like you've never known. As we choose to say, "With God, I can," we can expect Him to show up and be our daily portion of everything we need. Don't be afraid of the outcome; that's in God's hands. You just rest in the delight that walking with God this way is what your soul was designed for. The more you experience God, the more you expect to see and hear from Him every day. Obedience stops being a dutiful obligation and starts becoming a delight you crave.

When a woman says yes to God, she discovers a thrilling way to live.

Bible Study

Write your thoughts on this statement from this chapter:

> If our desire for obedience is born merely out of duty, we may be quick to give up. However, if our desire is born out of delight, out of a love relationship that burns deep in our soul, it won't be extinguished—no matter the cost.

What does serving God out of duty look like?

What does serving God out of delight look like?

Psalm 37:3-4 says,

> "Trust in the LORD and do good; dwell in the land and enjoy safe pasture. Delight yourself in the LORD and he will give you the desires of your heart."

Where will we find safety?

What will you be given as a result of delighting in the Lord?

How will the desires of our heart change as a result of having a love relationship with God?

Think about a tough situation you've faced recently. Write out a brief recount of this experience and identify the three things we learned when God says no.

Provision

Protection

Process

What are some of the "I can'ts" in your life right now?

Second Corinthians 12:8-10 says,

> Three times I pleaded with the Lord to take it away from me. But he said to me, "My grace is sufficient for you, for my power is made perfect in weakness." Therefore I will boast all the more gladly about my weaknesses, so that Christ's power may rest on me. That is why, for Christ's sake, I delight in weaknesses, in insults, in hardships, in persecutions, in difficulties. For when I am weak, then I am strong.

Do these verses give you an excuse to remain weak and subject to your "I can't"? Or do they tell you where you can draw strength from?

How do we tap into the strength of the Lord and use it to help us?

Romans 8:14-16 says,

> Those who are led by the Spirit of God are sons of God. For you did not receive a spirit that makes you a slave again to fear, but you received the Spirit of sonship. And by him we cry, "Abba, Father." The Spirit himself testifies with our spirit that we are God's children.

What does it look like to be led by the Spirit?

What is the promise of these verses, and how does it encourage you?

7

Keeping Our Vision Clear

Our life will follow where we focus our vision.

MY HUSBAND AND I found ourselves blessed with a little extra money once, and I started dreaming of new kitchen curtains. I stood in the kitchen and envisioned beautiful toile fabric cascading down and around my windows. I was so excited. I pleaded with my less-than-enthusiastic-about-the-curtains husband to understand that a woman's home is an expression of who she is, that curtains are important to the overall happiness I feel in my home. I even went so far as to pull out some handy-dandy Scriptures straight from Proverbs 31! I showed Art how this biblical woman made coverings for her bed, and I was sure she made matching window treatments as well.

Art still wasn't convinced. He kept gently telling me he felt led to give the money to ministry.

Ministry! Our whole lives were dedicated to ministry! "Honey," I countered, "I will have so much more to offer if only I feel complete and refreshed in our home. Did I mention that the home is the way a woman expresses her God-given creativity?"

My arguments, however, were not working. Eventually, my countenance turned sour and my words turned cold and flat toward my husband.

"Look, Lysa," Art finally said, exasperated, "if it's that big of a deal, we'll get the curtains."

I had won! You'd think I'd be overcome with joy and glee, but I caught a glimpse of my face in our bathroom mirror. It wasn't happy. It was harsh and pinched. I wasn't about to be deterred, though. I just needed a little makeup and all would be well. I reached underneath my sink where I keep my makeup bag, and it was gone. Then I felt God speak to my heart. He told me no amount of makeup was going to help what was wrong with me, and He would not allow me to find my makeup until I got back on track.

What? I asked Him in disbelief. *Don't You have some terrorists to round up? Or some hardened criminal to convict?* It was ridiculous to think that God would hide my makeup, so I determined to prove how crazy this was by finding my bag. I searched the entire house and both of our cars. I looked high and I looked low, and my makeup was nowhere to be found.

During my great hide-and-seek game, I continued to hear God's still, small voice speaking to me. As He tugged and prodded and convicted, I came to realize that my harsh facial expression was reflective of something ugly in my heart. My desire about what to do with the money had been all about me, me, me! Never once did I stop to pray. Instead, I pushed on with my agenda. Never once did I stop to consider the beautiful thing God was doing in my husband's heart by giving him the desire to share more abundantly. Never once did I take a step back to consider God's bigger picture and plan.

Was there anything wrong with new curtains? No. Was there anything wrong with my heart? Oh, yes. I had closed my heart to what

God wanted, to His calling. I had limited my vision to new curtains and, had it stayed there, that's all I may have been blessed with. But if I took hold of His vision, the Lord gently reminded me, how much more would my life be blessed?

That night when Art came in from work, I humbly went before him and told him how wrong it was that I had been so self-centered. With tears in my eyes, I apologized for not stopping long enough to consider what he and God wanted. Art accepted my apology, and suddenly I knew where my makeup was. Even though I had already thoroughly searched Art's car, I asked if he would go look once more. When he did, he found the makeup bag on the passenger floorboard—in plain sight.

God's Bigger, Grander Vision

Why is it that we can be so nearsighted when it comes to God's plans for us? Why do we let what's right in front of us distract us from the bigger, grander vision God has in mind?

To be radically obedient is to keep God's vision clearly in front of us, to be so busy looking at what He wants, looking at *Him,* that everything else becomes less important.

C.S. Lewis describes it as looking at "something beyond":

> I think all Christians would agree with me if I said that though Christianity seems at first to be all about morality, all about duties and guilt and virtue, yet it leads you on, out of all of that, into something beyond. One has a glimpse of a country where they do not talk of those things, except perhaps as a joke. Everyone there is filled with light. But they do not call it goodness. They do not call it anything. They are not thinking of it. They are too busy looking for the source from which it comes.[1]

Oh, Lord, give me the desire to be too busy looking at You to consider anything but Your plan! Strip away my short and narrow vision to see the wonderful adventure of truly being Your follower. Help me to be like Your disciples who followed immediately and fully rather than like the people who simply played games at the foot of Your cross.

How easy it is to obey partially. Obeying just enough to give the right Christian appearance is not the obedience God desires. He looks past all the outside trappings and misguided intentions straight to the heart. He wants our full attention and absolute devotion. Don't mistake this to look like a bunch of Christianese-speaking robots walking around chanting the rules of God. No, women who say yes to God are as unique in their approach to the sold-out life for Christ as pebbles found creekside. We've all been tumbled and smoothed in different ways, but we all have one thing in common...we know we rest in the mighty hand of God. Right now we may simply be an unsuspecting rock, but at anytime God could use us to slay the mightiest of giants. We live in anticipation and expectation of God showing up and giving evidence of how very near He always is.

I heard my local Christian radio station quoting Billy Graham the other day as once saying, "We can't see the wind, but we can feel its effects. In the same way, we can't see God, but we certainly see His effects." How true. The only thing I'd add to this fabulous quote is that the more we become aware of God's effects, the more we'll take credit away from happenstance and place it where it belongs, with God.

A few months ago I was praying specifically for God to reveal His activity in each of my children's lives. I knew they were Christians, but I wanted to see that they each had their own personal relationship with Him. I wanted God to be less about our family tradition and more about their own experience of Him. In little ways I started to see evidence of God's activity and discipleship springing to life in each of my kids. But the one that really captured my heart and burned a lasting impression in my soul was with my daughter Ashley.

I was speaking at a Ruth Graham and Friends conference out in California. While setting up my book table in the lobby of the church,

Ashley called me on my cell phone. Immediately, I sensed the heavy emotion in her tone as she tearfully said, "Mom, I need you to pray for me." I stopped what I was doing and walked outside. I assured her I would absolutely pray for her throughout the weekend but that I'd love to pray with her right that minute. I then inquired about what was troubling her. Her answer stunned me.

She was asking for me to pray that she would have the strength to continue a fast she'd started that morning. Two little boys from her school had recently lost their dad to cancer. She told me that God had clearly spoken to her heart that morning and challenged her to pray and fast for that family all day. She did exactly what God had told her to do but now her stomach was really hurting and she was having a hard time.

I checked my watch and calculated that it would be around 9 PM East Coast time. I encouraged her that sometimes God just intends a fast to be from sunup to sundown and that I was sure He'd be fine with her eating a little something before going to bed. She replied back, "Mom, I know exactly what God told me to do and I want to be obedient. I did not call for you to talk me out of this. I just need for you to pray for me to have the strength to continue."

Just then a wind blew that tousled my hair and my soul. Effects of God. Just what I'd been praying for. Ashley got it! She was more concerned about keeping God's vision clearly in front of her. She was so busy looking at what He wants, looking at *Him,* that everything else became less important.

By the time I walked back into that speaking engagement, I looked like a wreck. My hair was windblown, my makeup tear streaked, and my countenance emotional. But my soul was overflowing with the joyful knowledge that my precious daughter was becoming a true disciple, a young woman who says yes to God!

True Disciples vs. the Game Players

Two New Testament accounts from the life of Jesus contrast the true disciples from the game players. First, we find Simon Peter:

> He [Jesus] saw at the water's edge two boats, left there by the fishermen, who were washing their nets. He got into one of the boats, the one belonging to Simon, and asked him to put out a little from shore. Then he sat down and taught the people from the boat. When he had finished speaking, he said to Simon, "Put out into deep water, and let down the nets for a catch" (Luke 5:2-4).

Did you notice that there were two boats on the shore that day, and Jesus specifically chose Simon Peter's boat? Why? Because Jesus knew Simon Peter had a radically obedient heart and would be willing to do what He asked him—even when it made no sense. I like Peter's response to Jesus' request: "Master, we've worked hard all night and haven't caught anything. But because you say so, I will let down the nets" (verse 5). Do you hear what Peter is saying? "Though I'm tired from working all night, though I don't think You know much about fishing, Jesus, though it makes no sense at all in human terms… because You say so, I will do it."

How many times have I found myself in Peter's position and *not* responded in obedience the way he did? It saddens my heart to remember the occasions I've ignored Jesus' call for my radical obedience because I was tired, or because I didn't really believe Jesus would work miraculously in a particular situation, or mostly because the Lord's request made no sense in human terms.

I often wonder now at the blessings I've missed because of my lack of obedience. Look at what happened to Peter because of his obedience:

> When they had [let the nets down], they caught such a large number of fish that their nets began to break. So they signaled

their partners in the other boat to come and help them, and they came and filled both boats so full that they began to sink. When Simon Peter saw this, he fell at Jesus' knees and said, "Go away from me, Lord; I am a sinful man!" For he and all his companions were astonished at the catch of fish they had taken, and so were James and John, the sons of Zebedee, Simon's partners (Luke 5:6-10).

But Simon Peter's blessing that day didn't end with a huge catch of fish. His radical obedience to Jesus' simple request ultimately resulted in him discovering the calling on his life.

Then Jesus said to Simon, "Don't be afraid; from now on you will catch men." So they pulled their boats up on shore, left everything and followed him (Luke 5:10-11).

We have to remember that Simon Peter didn't know that something as mundane as lowering his net into the water would change his life—but it did! And that's how it can be for us. Our calling is revealed as we walk in daily obedience to Christ in the little things.

That's what's remarkable about radical obedience. You don't know where it will lead. You don't know how God will use it. That's what I love about Peter's story. It shows us so much about the radically obedient life.

First, as Peter discovered, *our call to obedience may challenge our pride*. God hates a prideful attitude (James 4:6). Many times the little steps leading to the bigger steps in our calling will be tests that help whittle the pride out of our heart. Peter, for instance, could have easily questioned Jesus' fishing knowledge…after all, Peter was a professional fisherman and Jesus was a carpenter. But Peter chose to swallow his pride and take the small step of obedience.

Second, *God uses our experiences to equip us for our calling*. God doesn't waste our experiences in life. I know in my own life God has been able to weave everything together to form a beautiful tapestry of good experiences, bad experiences, hurtful things, joyous things, professional jobs, ministry jobs, and everything else to prepare me for the work He is in the process of revealing to me. The same was true for Simon Peter. Yesterday he was fishing for fish; today he would be fishing for men.

Third, *our obedience may inspire others to respond.* What a radical blessing! As we respond in obedience, others will catch the vision and respond to God's calling on their own lives. Think of it. It wasn't just Peter's life that changed that day. The lives of his fishing partners, James and John, were never the same either. And it started with Peter saying yes to Jesus.

One caution at this point. We need to be careful not to fall into the trap of thinking that our blessings for radical obedience will profit our accounts and fill our pockets. Yes, Peter got a boatload of fish as a result of his obedience, but notice what he did: "So they pulled their boats up on shore, left everything and followed him" (Luke 5:11). They didn't celebrate their banner fishing day. They didn't consider the fish a just reward for all their hard work. They didn't sell the fish and use the money to buy more boats and hang out a new shingle announcing their expanded fishing fleet. No, they were only thinking of the person who allowed it to happen—and they left it all behind and followed Him. Sounds a lot like that C.S. Lewis quote. "They do not call it anything. They are not thinking of it. They are too busy looking for the source from which it comes."

Where We Focus Our Vision

Now contrast Peter's story with another incident we find recorded in Luke:

Jesus said, "Father, forgive them, for they do not know what they are doing." And they divided up his clothes by casting lots (Luke 23:34).

It's hard to imagine anyone playing games in the shadow of the cross while the Savior of the world looked on in excruciating pain. He was dying for their sins, and they were dying for one good roll of the dice. They didn't even hear His cry for God to forgive them. They missed His offer of eternal significance because they were too distracted by earthly rags. They had no vision beyond the moment. Max Lucado writes of this scene:

> It makes me think of us...I'm thinking that we are not so unlike those soldiers. We, too, play games at the foot of the cross. We compete for members. We scramble for status. We deal out judgments and condemnations. Competition. Selfishness. Personal gain. It's all there...So close to the timber yet so far from the blood.[2]

Are we like Peter? Or are we like these soldiers at the foot of the cross? Our life will follow where we choose to focus our vision. If we are serious about radical obedience, about having a vision that's God inspired, then we must keep our focus on Christ. When Christ speaks, we must listen. When He directs us to act, we must act. When He compels us to give, we must do so freely. When He reminds us to get past trivial matters, we must let our pride fall away. When He invites us to leave the world behind, we must follow Him.

For Peter, it was a net full of fish. For me, it was those kitchen curtains. You'll probably be happy to hear that I did eventually get new kitchen curtains. But they are not the lovely, feminine ones I always thought I wanted.

A few years before we adopted our sons from Africa, Art was invited to participate in the hunting expedition of a lifetime. He and several of his friends traveled to South Africa to hunt wild beasts with bows and arrows. I have to admit, I was not happy about this little adventure, but I knew that Art desperately wanted to go. God softened me by whispering a promise to my heart that if I let Art go on this manly excursion, it would be a big way that I could give Art the respect he needed from his wife. I sent off my rough-and-tumble husband only to welcome him home two weeks later a changed man.

He brought me back some beautifully written love letters—I could hardly believe he penned them himself. He brought back pictures of the award-winning warthog he'd taken as well as other animals I'd never heard of in my life. Then he proudly announced that several of these stuffed beasts would soon be residing as prize mounts in our home. Needless to say, my lovely floral, toile, and girly plaid decor soon gave way to more of a *Survivor* theme. Pinks, greens, blues, and yellows gave way to earth tones and our traditional white woodwork was stripped, stained, and even replaced in some areas with cedar and stone accents.

Those lovely toile kitchen curtains that I fought for, agonized over, and felt so deprived in not getting would have been a complete waste. They would either be collecting dust in my attic or be in a trash bag labeled "garage sale" and taking up space in the garage. The rustic brown curtains that adorn my kitchen now are not at all what I envisioned but just the right accent to my now earthy kitchen. I have to admit that I hardly notice my kitchen curtains, but when I do I smile. Not because of their decorator appeal, although I really do like them, but rather because of the funny way that even in something as simple as curtains for your home, you can experience God. That is, if you choose to. Truly, a woman who says yes to God knows that her life will follow where she focuses her vision.

Bible Study

In several of my recent books I've made comments about my dog, Champ, whom I love dearly, though I'm not a real "dog person." But usually my comments are centered in his misguided desire to run away from home. Though we've installed an Invisible Fence, he will sometimes take the pain of a shock just to live free and dangerous for a while. I was lamenting to my friend Holly abut how much this breaks my heart. Champ has a great home where all his needs are met and where he is loved to pieces, so why would he run? With great wisdom she replied, "Lysa, he simply lives in the moment." That's it! He doesn't think beyond what he wants right this minute. He has no thoughts beyond the moment; therefore, he has no vision for what's best for his life. Think about one of the key points from this chapter: "Her life will follow where she focuses her vision." How does this statement challenge you personally?

Are you sometimes guilty of sacrificing what you want most for what you want right now? For example: I want a great relationship with God, but I want to sleep in more right now. So, once again I sacrifice my time with the Lord for a few more minutes of sleep. Or, I want to lose weight, but I want this piece of chocolate cake more right now.

So, once again I satisfy my tastebuds and sacrifice my desire to be more healthy. Write your thoughts here.

In this chapter we discovered three truths about obedience.

The first truth: *Our call to obedience may challenge our* _____ (page 135).

Read James 4:4-6. What are these verses saying?

In *The Message* these verses read:

> You're cheating on God. If all you want is your own way, flirting with the world every chance you get, you end up enemies of God and his way. And do you suppose God doesn't care? The proverb has it that "he's a fiercely jealous lover." And what he gives in love is far better than anything else you'll find. It's common knowledge that "God goes against the willful proud; God gives grace to the willing humble."

Define "willful proud" and give an example of something you might be willfully proud about in your life right now.

Define "willing humble" and give an example of something you might be willingly humble about in your life right now.

The second truth: *God uses our* _____ *to equip us for our calling* (page 135).

Read Philippians 2:14-16. How are we to shine like stars in the universe? This same passage in *The Message* reads:

> Do everything readily and cheerfully—no bickering, no second-guessing allowed! Go out into the world uncorrupted, a breath of fresh air in this squalid and polluted society. Provide people with a glimpse of good living and of the living God. Carry the light-giving Message into the night so I'll have good cause to be proud of you on the day that Christ returns. You'll be living proof that I didn't go to all this work for nothing.

How can your life experiences help provide people with glimpses of God?

The third truth: *Our obedience may inspire* _____ *to respond* (page 136).

Read Luke 5:11. Who responded that day?

How does their response inspire you?

Fill in the blanks for the statement below pulled from this chapter (see page 137):

Are we like Peter? Or are we like these soldiers at the foot of the cross? Our life will follow where we choose to focus our _____. If we are serious about radical obedience, about having a vision that's God inspired, then we must keep our _____ on _____. When Christ speaks, we must _____. When He directs us to act, we must _____. When He compels us to _____, we must do so _____. When He reminds us to get past trivial matters, we must let our _____ fall away. When He invites us to leave the world behind, we must _____ Him.

Journal your thoughts about that paragraph here:

Giving Up What Was Never Ours

We are managers, not owners, of God's resources.

I WAS GOING THROUGH a fast-food drive-through one day when I realized I didn't have enough cash on me to pay for the lunch I'd ordered for my daughter Hope and myself. I knew Hope, who had just celebrated her ninth birthday, had received a ten-dollar bill as a gift from her aunt. I asked Hope if I could borrow just a few dollars to make up for my shortage, and I promised I would pay her back. She refused, explaining that she was seeing some of her friends that afternoon and wanted to show them her ten-dollar bill. It just would not be the same to show them a five-dollar bill and a couple of ones. No, she insisted, she had to keep her ten-dollar bill for herself.

I asked her if she trusted that I would pay her back. She said she did, but I might not pay her back with a ten-dollar bill. She did not want two fives. She did not want ten ones. She did not want any combination of bills. She wanted a ten. A ten-dollar bill would, after all, be much more impressive to her friends.

As it was approaching my turn at the drive-through window, I got more aggressive with my offer. I told her I would not only give her the change from her original ten-dollar bill, which was going to be about seven dollars, but that I would also give her another ten-dollar bill later. Even this offer was not enough to release her tight grip on her beloved bill. She did not want a ten-dollar bill later because she might miss showing off to her friends today.

Did my sweet daughter not realize that I had the ability to bless her with many ten-dollar bills? Did she not appreciate the fact that I had just spent the equivalent of more than ten ten-dollar bills on her birthday party? Did she even have a clue as to how many ten-dollar bills I've spent on her over her lifetime? Not to mention the fact that her lunch was part of the reason I was spending this ten-dollar bill at the moment?

Finally, when we were at the window, Hope begrudgingly gave me the money. How it disappointed me that she would not willingly release the ten-dollar bill.

How it must disappoint God when we do this very same thing.

You see, I had special knowledge that Hope did not have. I knew that waiting in our mailbox at home was another birthday card—one from her grandmother that contained a whopping fifty dollars! Her ten-dollar bill would pale in comparison.

Likewise, God has special knowledge in our lives. He has blessings for the radically obedient that make the dime-store stuff we are so intent on holding on to pale in comparison. The question is, do we trust Him? Do we trust that He will bless us? Do we trust that His blessings are infinitely better than what He might first ask us to release?

The Floodgates of Blessing

Trust. Isn't that why more of us don't offer all we have to God? We don't trust that He really will throw open the floodgates of blessing in return.

"Bring the whole tithe into the storehouse, that there may be food in my house. Test me in this," says the LORD Almighty, "and see if I will not throw open the floodgates of heaven and pour out so much blessing that you will not have room enough for it" (Malachi 3:10).

Sacrificial giving is one of the few times God asks us to test Him. Yet for many years I found myself unwilling to accept the challenge. I was willing to tithe but not willing to go beyond what I felt comfortable giving. Leaving our comfort zone, however, is the very place God calls us to. He wants us to venture into truly abundant giving. He wants us to get out from under our own selfishness with our possessions and accept His invitation to become radically obedient with what we own. Then, not only will He bless us, but He will lavish blessing upon blessing on us.

I saw this firsthand when I was saving money for a new outfit. I started this "new outfit fund" because of an embarrassing situation I found myself in during a country club speaking engagement. I was wearing what I thought was a very nice outfit. When I showed up at the event, however, I quickly realized that not only was my outfit a little out of style, but my white discount store shoes were the only light-colored foot apparel in the entire building. (Not being a queen of fashion, I was unaware of the rule that white shoes have to wait until after Memorial Day in some parts of the country.) Everyone had on dark-colored shoes, so with every step I took, I felt as though my feet were screaming, "White shoes! Everyone look at my shocking white shoes!"

You'll be happy to know that not even white shoes could stop me from sharing about Jesus with this lovely group of women, but you'd better believe I was determined to update and improve my wardrobe.

It took me a while, but I managed to save up one hundred dollars in my "new outfit fund," so I set a date to go shopping with some of my fashion-savvy friends. Just a few days before I was to go shopping, another dear friend phoned to ask me to pray for her family's financial situation. They could not make ends meet and had many bills they were unable to pay. She mentioned they needed one hundred dollars immediately. While she was only asking me to pray for her and nothing more, I knew God was looking for a response from me that would honor Him. I prayed for my friend and I obeyed God's prompting to give to her the money I'd saved.

The day arrived for my shopping trip, and I must admit that instead of being excited, I felt a pang of dread. I knew that because I had given my money away, I could only look and not purchase anything. I didn't want my fashion friends to think I was wasting their time, so I decided I would put whatever clothes they picked out for me on hold and pray that God would provide the means to return later and purchase them.

While I was moping about and strategizing, God was at work in my friends' hearts. After trying on three beautiful outfits complete with shoes and accessories, I returned to my dressing room to try and decide which outfit to put on hold. While I dressed, my friends took everything to the checkout counter and treated me to a $700 shopping spree!

"Test me in this," says the LORD Almighty, "and see if I will not throw open the floodgates of heaven and pour out so much blessing that you will not have room for it." I was shocked and humbled that God had taken the little gift I'd given to my friend and returned it sevenfold through other friends.

The Life That Is Truly Life

The apostle Paul wrote:

> Command those who are rich in this present world not to be arrogant nor to put their hope in wealth, which is so uncertain, but to put their hope in God, who richly provides us with everything for our enjoyment. Command them to do good, to be rich in good deeds, and to be generous and willing to share. In this

way they will lay up treasure for themselves as a firm foundation for the coming age, so that they may take hold of the life that is truly life (1 Timothy 6:17-19).

In this country, I think we would agree that most of us are "rich" and this passage applies to us. So, what motivates us to venture out into the area of sacrificial giving—an area that for many of us is a real stretch? There are two radical blessings tucked within Paul's words here. The first, which is also referenced in Matthew 6, speaks of laying up treasures in heaven—sending that which we cannot take with us ahead where we can enjoy it and benefit from it in eternity. If you knew you could immediately enjoy a treasure for one day or enjoy it forever if you waited just a short while, which would you choose? In this light, the eternal route makes so much more sense.

The second blessing goes hand in hand with the first. God is aware of our humanness and our desire for instant gratification. He tends to that as well. Not only are we blessed for eternity when we give, but we are blessed for today too: "So that they may take hold of the life that is truly life."

To live life that is "truly life" is to live abundantly in the here and now.

In his book *The Treasure Principle*, Randy Alcorn wrote:

> The act of giving is a vivid reminder that it's all about God, not about us. It's saying I am not the point, *He* is the point. He does not exist for me. I exist for Him. God's money has a higher purpose than my affluence. Giving is a joyful surrender to a greater person and a greater agenda. Giving affirms Christ's lordship. It dethrones me and exalts Him. It breaks the chains of mammon that would enslave me. As long as I still have something, I believe I own it. But when I give it away, I relinquish control, power and prestige. At the moment of release the light turns on. The magic spell is broken. My mind clears. I recognize God as owner, myself

as servant, and others as intended beneficiaries of what God has entrusted to me.[1]

If we choose to obey and give of our resources in abundance, a feeling of amazing satisfaction will follow. The radical blessing of being able to take hold of a real life—a fulfilled and satisfied life we can't find any other way—will be ours.

Just Give Me Five Minutes

Dane and Kema Kovach are friends of ours who just a few years ago seemed as though they were on the fast track to the American Dream. Dane was an orthodontist with a thriving practice. He was a dedicated family man, leader in our church, and avid outdoorsman. Kema was a terrific mother of four precious adopted children and busy making plans to build their dream home. They had land, architectural drawings, and beautiful decorating plans. Just a few months before they were to break ground, our church started a building campaign that would allow us to move from our temporary high school auditorium home to a real building we could call our own.

During this campaign many amazing stories of sacrifice began to surface within the families of our church. The Kovaches were no exception. God began stirring in Dane's and Kema's hearts individually. Both were nervous about sharing with the other the absolute radical direction they felt God leading them in. Just a few weeks before the commitment ceremony, where the leaders of the church promised the firstfruits of the building offering, they both sheepishly approached a conversation they had to have. Imagine their shock as they realized God was speaking to both of them about sacrificing the money they'd saved for their dream home.

Joyfully, they placed their dreams in God's hands and invested their finances for eternity.

This act set their hearts on fire for God. Never did I see Dane and Kema after that where the joy of the Lord didn't just radiate off them. It wasn't long afterward that Dane went on a mission trip only to return with another shocking revelation from God: Both Dane and Kema felt they were being called to the mission field.

Just before they left, they proudly stood before our congregation and gave some insights from their amazing adventure with God during the years leading up to their departure for Papua New Guinea.

Dane was quick to give an answer to the questions swirling about them during their time of preparation to leave. "When people ask me why I'm doing all this, selling my thriving practice, taking my family of six on the mission field for four years, giving up what most consider the American Dream, I have to point to the overwhelming joy and fulfillment I feel at this point in my life in my relationship with the Lord. I only wish I could place my heart inside the person questioning me and let them experience this joy that I feel for just five minutes."

I have a feeling that if Dane could do this, our world would look like a dramatically different place. Our thinking is so upside down. We fear that giving sacrificially will make our lives empty, when in reality withholding is what leads to emptiness. Giving, releasing, surrendering to God in this way, is what leads to more fulfillment than we ever dreamed possible.

Seeing Beyond Our Own Mailbox

I must admit that sometimes I am tempted to become consumed with all the ministry opportunities just within the walls of the Ter-Keurst home. Having five kids can be a delightful but daunting task at times. Yet while my family is my primary ministry, it is not my only ministry.

God has placed the desire in my heart to reach out past my mailbox, past myself, and look for opportunities to live a sacrificial life that touches others for Christ. While God has not called me to the mission field on foreign soil, He has called me to a life of mission work in this place He has me now. Sometimes these "others" I'm called to reach out to are complete strangers whom I touch for a moment and pray God will use me to draw their hearts closer to Him. Other times the opportunities I'm blessed with are with people I know and come in contact with often enough to see God's bigger plan after I play my small role. Such was the case with my dear friend Genia one evening as we gathered with a couple of our close friends for dinner.

Genia and I are part of a small group of very close friends. We call our group "ASAP," which stands for Accountability, Sharing our dreams, Asking the tough questions, and Praying for one another. One night during our meeting, Genia was sharing a tough place she found herself in. As she described her situation, it reminded me of a song on my favorite CD. The Christian artist who sang the song perfectly described what it is like to be caught between life before really living for Christ and life where you sense God leading. This longing to go back and yet the desire to move ahead into a deeper walk with Christ was the place my friend found herself. I knew I had to let Genia hear this song.

After dinner I asked Genia to walk to my car with me to listen to the CD. I was in the process of telling her how I had this CD on continual play in my car because I loved it so much when God interrupted my thoughts and told me to give Genia the CD.

As the song played, Genia had tears in her eyes and told me that it perfectly described how she was feeling. I pushed eject, placed the CD in its plastic case, and handed it to her. I told her that God wanted her to have this CD, so now it was hers. Instead of listening to the music as I made my way home that night, I sat in silent prayer for my friend. It was a beautiful ride home.

The next day, Genia called with such excitement in her voice that she could hardly contain herself. She said she had listened to the CD over and over. She had played it for her husband, who agreed it perfectly described their situation. Then she remembered something that brought her to her knees. Three weeks earlier she'd attended a special prayer service where a woman whom Genia did not know came over and prayed with her. The woman told Genia that God loved her, He understood where she was, He promised not to leave her, and that He would give her a song to minister to her. "A song, Lysa, a song!" she exclaimed. "God promised me a song, and He used your hands to deliver it last night."

Tears welled up in my eyes as I realized that what I thought was a simple gift had actually been a well-timed God event for my friend's life! But the blessing didn't end there. Later that same day, the vice president of a large ministry called me on my cell phone. She said God had given her an idea for special retreats to reach women all across the country. She told God that she would write down any names that came to her mind as possible leaders for these retreats. She took out a piece of paper and instantly three names came to mind. She wrote her own name at the top. She then wrote two other names that had really been on her heart: mine and the Christian artist of the CD I had given to Genia.

All I did was give away a CD.

The Blessings of a Sacrificial Life

Understanding and discovering the beautiful opportunities of sacrificial living is so opposite of what the world tells us, and yet it is the only way to find the happiness and joy our hearts long for. The apostle John put it this way:

Dear children, let us not love with words or tongue but with actions and in truth. This then is how we know that we belong to the truth, and how we set our hearts at rest in his presence (1 John 3:18-19).

I am convinced there is a treasure in life that very few find: a heart that is at rest in His presence. And how do we find this heart at rest? Through actions and in truth. I must confess I have moments where my heart is at rest in His presence, but they are broken up by pitfalls and pity parties. Sometimes I just simply want to be selfish. But when I choose selfishness, I may be happy for the moment, but I'm miserable in the long run.

Yet, my Lord, with His incredible patience, doesn't leave me in my misery. I call out to Him in repentance and, just like a connect-the-dots game, Jesus fills in the gaps between the dots to reveal a beautiful picture of Himself in my life. What if there were less and less space between my dots, revealing an even clearer picture of Christ in my life at all times? Oh, that it could be so. If only I could learn to practice the presence of Christ at every moment, in every decision, with all whom I come in contact. Setting my heart at rest in His presence in this way comes with practice and maturity. The more I practice His presence, the more I will experience His presence, and the more mature I will become.

Elizabeth George talks about the process of maturity in a beautiful way:

> The Old Testament term for the word gentleness, *anah,* describes a mature, ripened shock of grain with its head bent low and bowed down. Just think for a moment on the beauty of this word picture. As wheat grows, the young sprouts rise above the rest. Their heads shoot up the highest because no grain has yet formed. In their immaturity, little fruit, if any, has appeared. But, as time passes and maturity sets in, fruit comes forth—so much of it that the burdened stalk bends and its head sinks lower and lower—and the lower the head the greater amount of fruit.[2]

Lord, help me to lower my head past my selfishness and pride, past desiring others to serve me and on to serving others, past wanting more and on to giving more, past me in search of You. Help me to always desire the lowered head, full of Your fruit and consumed with Your presence. Help me to be forever mindful of my ministry at home as well as the ministry opportunities that wait beyond my own mailbox.

God owns it all. We are simply managers of His resources. When we pursue the beautiful opportunities of sacrificial living, we freely acknowledge that truth and then reap the blessings. When we come to understand that we're giving up what was never ours to begin with, we're walking in radical obedience.

Bible Study

Read Psalm 81:8-16. Now let's break down some of the verses to unearth the rich treasures contained within. First, look at verse 9:

> "You shall have no foreign god among you; you shall not bow down to an alien god."

Though our hearts are not often tempted to bow down to statues and gods of other religions, we are often tempted to bow down to other things. Write some things that tempt us to pull our focus off God.

Though we may not physically get on the floor and bow to these things, when we give them so much attention that they take priority over the things of God in our life, it's problematic. Also, when we hold on to these things so tightly that to be asked to release them causes great turmoil in our spirit, that is a sign of trouble. And don't mistake the fact that these things in and of themselves may not even be bad things. They might be good things. But as Jim Collins in his business book called *Good to Great* points out, sometimes the enemy to great is often settling for good. Write a description of what many consider to be the "good life."

Now contrast that with what God would define as "the great life."

Read verse 10 from Psalm 81:

> "I am the LORD your God, who brought you up out of Egypt.
> Open wide your mouth and I will fill it."

There are three key points from this verse. First, a reminder of the fact that the Lord is our God. Why is it important for us to keep that in the forefront of our minds?

Second, He is our God, who has been faithful throughout our journey and delivered us. What does this mean to you personally?

Third, if we open ourselves up to Him fully, He will fill us. What does opening ourselves up to Him fully mean?

What will God fill us with?

Verse 16 says:

> "You would be fed with the finest of wheat; with honey from the rock I would satisfy you."

What does temporary satisfaction look like?

What does real satisfaction look like?

Do you believe God is capable of truly satisfying you?

Verses 11 and 12 warn us about being self-focused, close-fisted, and stubborn-hearted: "My people would not listen to me; Israel would not submit to me. So I gave them over to their stubborn hearts to follow their own devices." What were the consequences for the Israelites not listening to God, not trusting God, and constantly complaining to God? Find an example in the Old Testament of Israel following their own devices and suffering because of it. If you are having a hard time knowing where to start, look in Numbers 11:1,4; 14:1-4; or 20:2-3. List their complaint, their sin, and their consequence.

In this chapter we read,

> "Dear children, let us not love with words or tongue but with actions and in truth. This then is how we know that we belong to the truth, and how we set our hearts at rest in his presence" (1 John 3:18-19).

How do you plan to apply this verse to your life?

What is the promise in store for the person who applies this truth?

9

Radically Blessed

The blessings of radical obedience are unending.

THE OTHER DAY I WAS DRIVING down a busy road when I came upon a traffic light that was both green and red at the same time. I slowed, unsure of what I should do, as did other cars coming from all directions. It was a confusing and dangerous situation. Some people stopped, others ran through the light, and still others pulled off to the side of the intersection.

I finally made it through the intersection and thought about this unusual happening. It was as if God were showing me a visual picture of what it's like when a person is indecisive in her obedience to Him. We can't seek to follow God wholeheartedly if part of our heart is being pulled in a different direction. We can't pursue the radically obedient life and still continue to flirt with disobedience in certain areas of our life. We can't be both red and green toward God at the same time. It gets us nowhere. It's confusing. It's dangerous.

This book has been your invitation to become a woman who says yes to God and catches a glimpse of the blessings that are ahead. Now it's time to respond.

Don't be afraid, my friend. I know your mind might be flooded with the same questions that flooded my mind as I was responding to this invitation.

"What if I don't feel able to make such a commitment?"

"What if I say yes and then mess up?"

"What if I have times when I just don't feel like being obedient?"

Let's go back to my husband's sage advice: Consider the source. Who is asking these questions? That's not your voice sowing seeds of doubt; it's Satan's voice. He wants to keep you in doubt and confusion. He wants you to pull off to the side of the intersection and remain ineffective. He wants you to fail to fulfill the purposes God has for you and thwart the positive impact you could make in the lives of so many.

You don't feel able? Good! Christ's power is made perfect through weakness (2 Corinthians 12:9). Ask God for the strength to persevere every day. Ask God for the desire to remain radically obedient and for spiritual eyes to see the radical blessings He will shower upon you.

What if you mess up? Grace! "God opposes the proud but gives grace to the humble. Submit yourselves, then, to God. Resist the devil, and he will flee from you. Come near to God and he will come near to you...humble yourselves before the Lord, and he will lift you up" (James 4:6-8,10). Please don't think I walk this radical obedience journey with perfection, because I don't. Chances are you won't either. But God doesn't expect perfection from us—He expects a person humble enough to admit her weaknesses and committed enough to press through and press on. He will guide us past the doubts and fears and lift us up to fulfill our calling.

What if you wake up in a bad mood and just don't feel like being obedient? Choice! Obey based on your decision to obey, not on your ever-changing feelings. *I don't feel like giving. I don't feel like smiling. I don't feel like listening to God.* But here's what God has to say about that: "It is *God* who works in you to will and to act according to his good purpose" (Philippians 2:13, emphasis added). When we ask God to continually give us the desire to remain obedient, He does. He will help us to want to obey Him and will give us His power to do so.

Get Ready!

If your answer is no to radical obedience, then let it be no. I just ask you to do one thing while you sit at the red light. Pray that God will give you the desire to say yes. Let me challenge you for the next 30 days to pray and ask God to reveal Himself to you and fill you with a desire for Him like never before. Remember that lasting obedience must be born out of desire, not duty. Choose to be a woman who says yes to God by starting with this simple prayer. It will cost you only a minute of your time each day, but it will bless you for a lifetime!

If your answer to this invitation is yes, then get ready. You have not only signed up for the most incredible journey you can imagine, but you've also just given God the green light to pour out His radical blessings on your life! What I'm writing about here is just a glimpse of how God will bless you. He's capable of so much more!

Deeper Relationship with God

You will begin to live in expectation of hearing from God every day. You will start to better understand His character and seek to be more like Him. You will discover the depth of love that the Father has for you that you never even knew was possible. This will give you a feeling of acceptance and significance that you can't get any other way.

Some people spend their whole lives chasing things they think will make them feel accepted and significant. But the truth is this world only has packages full of empty promises to offer. The new house, the fancier car, the latest gadget, the fastest computer, the sleek fashions, and everything else that seems so enticing won't last. They will all wear out, break down, tear up, and become obsolete. Five, ten, twenty years from now, they won't look so appealing and will have to either be updated or replaced. Fifty years from now, most will be taking up space in a junkyard somewhere.

In contrast, every investment we make in our relationship with God will only serve to reap rich dividends for now and eternity. No time spent experiencing God will ever be a waste.

More Adventurous Life

I've heard it said that life would not be so hard if it weren't so daily. Yet the Bible says that each day is a gift from God that we should rejoice in (Psalm 118:24). Daily adventures with God will add an excitement to your life that will change your whole perspective. No longer is your day just one humdrum task after another, but rather a string of divine appointments and hidden treasures waiting to be discovered.

Seeing life like this opens up God's storehouses of joy. The mark of a truly godly woman is one who reveals the power of God not so much in her doing as in her being. She has opened God's treasure chest of joy and so filled her heart with gratitude and love that just being around her inspires you. She goes about the simplest of tasks, her everyday duties, and even the rough patches of life with such grace that you find yourself wanting to imitate her. She is full of adventure yet not worn out from the journey.

Depth of Inner Peace

In our world of turmoil and uncertainty, there is nothing more precious than peace. When we say yes to God, we know that our life and the lives of those we love rest in the certainty of His never-changing love for us. While we can't control the circumstances we face, we can choose how we react to them. If you've settled in your heart to say yes to God and completely trust Him, then you don't have to worry about the future. You are not in charge of the outcome, you are simply responsible to be obedient. You will be blessed with the peace of knowing that God has a perfect plan and holds everything in His perfect control. What freedom this brings!

Personal Satisfaction

Radically obedient people no longer have to strategize and manipulate things into being. Instead, they are blessed with opportunities that bring them real satisfaction according to God's perfect design for them. When my husband and I adopted our sons from Liberia, I thought the responsibility of adding more children would mean the end of my ministry. But that has not been the case. God has grown the ministry, sent more people to help run it, and blessed us with the most amazing opportunities to tell our adoption story. We've been allowed to freely talk about listening and obeying God on *Good Morning America, The Oprah Winfrey Show,* and in *O, The Oprah Magazine.* God has taken our obedience and maximized our ministry's impact.

Better Relationships with People

In every relationship with others, you will find things that you love and things that, to be quite honest, get on your nerves. The radically obedient person is blessed with being able to appreciate another's Christlikeness and to give grace to their humanness. Whether a person is a believer or not, he is still made in God's image, and God is crazy in love with him. When you are committed to radical obedience, you see everyone through God's eyes of love.

Meaning and Purpose to Life

Author Bruce Wilkinson wrote:

Radically obedient people no longer have to strategize and manipulate things into being. Instead, they are blessed with opportunities that bring them real satisfaction according to God's perfect design for them.

Once the Lord has fed His child through intimate devotions, He begins to call him more pointedly to deeper obedience. At this point, the believer desires more of the Lord so much that he is more than willing to do whatever the Lord requires…Obedience for this individual is no longer a burden, undertaken only because the Bible tells him to do something. Rather, obedience becomes a joy because his closest friend and most compassionate Lord beckons him to be like Him.[1]

Our hearts search for deeper meaning in life, and radically obedient people find it in loving the Lord, loving others He brings in our path, and continually seeking to become more like Jesus.

Eternal Perspective

Life is about so much more than just the here and now, and the radically obedient person lives in light of that perspective. Life isn't about being comfortable and taking the easiest route. It's about living to give our lives away and making a real impact in this world. It's not about serving out of religious duty. It's about delighting in our relationship with God so much that we want to serve out of an overflow of love and gratitude. Our time here is but a small dot on an eternal line. What we do now in this brief moment will determine our destiny for eternity. The radically obedient person is blessed with an eternal perspective.

A Radically Obedient Example

I am drawn to the story of one New Testament woman who was radically obedient—Mary, Lazarus' sister. I am moved by Mary's overwhelming love for Jesus. She was a woman who understood the essence of radical obedience. She knew when to listen and when to act. She knew when to simply sit at the Master's feet and when to pour out all she had in lavish love for her Lord (Matthew 26:6-13).

Jesus had just announced He would be crucified. Mary took what

Life isn't about being comfortable and
taking the easiest route.
It's about living to give our lives away.

was probably her most costly possession, the perfume from her alabaster jar, and poured it out on Him. Normally, one would pour perfume on a dead body, but Mary anointed Jesus while He was still living. I believe it was so Jesus could carry the scent of her love with Him to the cross.

Mary was scolded by some of the disciples for her act of extravagance (naysayers!), but Jesus was quick to jump to her defense. What others saw as waste, Jesus saw as the purest form of walking out the gospel message. She was willing to love Him without reservation, without concern for what others might think or even concern for herself. Mary showed an unabashed love through this act, and, make no mistake, Jesus was quick to lavish His love right back on her. "I tell you the truth," Jesus said, "wherever the gospel is preached throughout the world, what she has done will also be told, in memory of her" (Matthew 26:13).

Isn't it amazing that such a small act of obedience could have such far-reaching effects? That can happen in our lives as well. Indeed, Mary was radically obedient and radically blessed...and you can be too.

How It Ends

Well, this whole adventure began with God telling me to give away my Bible, so is it any surprise that it ends the same way? Just last weekend I was flying to the Washington, DC, area for a speaking engagement. The man next to me on the plane was busy working on his computer and did not appear to be in the mood to be interrupted. My heart kept feeling drawn to share the gospel with him, but it didn't seem appropriate to force a conversation. So I prayed.

I prayed that God would prompt *him* to start talking to me. And talk he did. It wasn't long before he put his computer away and started asking me all kinds of questions about my career. Because I write and speak about Jesus, this was a perfect opportunity to tell him all about my Boss! When we started talking about God, he said he'd been studying the Koran and several other religious writings, but not the Bible. However, he'd called the friend he was traveling to see and asked if they could buy a Bible that weekend to complete his collection.

I almost fell out of my seat. Of all the planes traveling to Washington that day and of all the people who were seated together, God arranged for a man who needed a Bible to sit beside a woman who loves to give Bibles away! I shared with my new friend my passion for giving away Bibles, and I promised I would send him one the next week. He sat stunned. When he finally spoke again, he told me he knew this was more than sheer coincidence. He knew God was reaching out to him.

Oh, my friend, we don't have to seek to create opportunities to say yes to God. God has already gone before us and established them. We simply have to respond.

I pray that the end of this book is not the conclusion of your journey. I sincerely hope this is only the starting place, the point of inspiration and expression for you to live a radically obedient, radically blessed life. What happens when women say yes to God? The world is changed.

We don't have to seek to
create opportunities to say yes to God.
God has already gone
before us and established them.
We simply have to respond.

Bible Study

For this concluding Bible study we are going to do something a little different. God's Word has much to say on the topic of saying yes to God and the amazing blessings that follow. Pick ten of these key verses, look them up for yourself, and discover what God wants you to know about His calling on your life. I've summarized the verses, but it will be so much more powerful to dig into God's Word and record the powerful promises yourself.

Deuteronomy 28:1-14
Obedience opens God's storehouse of blessings.

2 Chronicles 16:9
God will strengthen the heart of the obedient person.

Esther 4:14
God has called you to obedience for such a time as this.

Psalm 15
Obedient people dwell in the presence and peace of God.

Psalm 24
Obedience in what you say, what you do, and what you think leads to holiness and blessings from God.

Isaiah 55:1-3

Obedience brings your soul
satisfaction, delight, and new life.

Hosea 10:12

Obedience reaps the fruit of unfailing love
and brings showers of righteousness.

Malachi 3:8-10

Being obedient givers will open
God's storehouse of blessing.

Malachi 3:16-17

Radically obedient people are treasures to God.

Matthew 26:12-13

Even small acts of obedience have widespread effects.

Romans 1:5

Obedience comes from faith.

Romans 6:15-16

Obedience leads to righteousness.

Romans 8:5-6

Those walking in obedience have their
minds set on God's desires.

2 Corinthians 9:6

The extent that we sow in obedience will determine the extent we will reap in blessings.

2 Corinthians 9:13

Men will praise God for the obedience that accompanies our faith.

Ephesians 4:24

We were created to be like God. We walk this out in obedience leading to holiness.

Philippians 2:13

It is God working in us that prompts us to be obedient and fulfill His good purpose.

Philippians 4:9

What you have learned, heard, or seen from God, walk it out in obedience and you will be blessed with peace.

2 Timothy 2:20-21

God is able to use the obedient person for His noblest purposes.

Hebrews 11

A list of radically obedient, radically blessed people.

1 Peter 1:13-14

Prepare your mind for obedience, which leads to holiness.

1 Peter 2:21-22

Those who walk in obedience walk in Jesus' footsteps.

1 John 2:3-6

Obedience makes God's love complete in us
and enables us to walk as Jesus did.

Notes

Chapter Two: Hearing God's Voice

1. *Life Application Study Bible (NIV)* (Wheaton, IL: Tyndale House Publishers, 1988), p. 2125.

2. Rick Warren, *The Purpose-Driven Life* (Grand Rapids, MI: Zondervan Publishing House, 2002), p. 233.

3. A.J. Russell, ed., *God Calling* (Grand Rapids, MI: Spire Books, 2005), p. 113.

Chapter Three: When Obedience Becomes Radical

1. *Life Application Study Bible (NIV)* (Wheaton, IL: Tyndale House Publishers, 1988), p. 1632.

Chapter Four: You Never Know How God Will Use You Until You Let Him

1. *Life Application Study Bible (NIV)* (Wheaton, IL: Tyndale House Publishers, 1998), p. 2277.

2. A.J. Russell, ed., *God Calling*, May 19.

3. "I Wonder Why," blog entry, July 18, 2006, written by Beverly Daffron. Used with permission.

Chapter Five: What Keeps Us from Saying Yes to God

1. Rick Warren, *The Purpose-Driven Life* (Grand Rapids, MI: Zondervan Publishing House, 2002), p. 254.

2. Beth Moore, *Living Free* (Nashville, TN: LifeWay Press, 2001), p. 82.

3. Ibid., p. 77.

Chapter Six: If It Were Easy, It Wouldn't Be Worth Doing

1. Brent Curtis and John Eldredge, *The Sacred Romance* (Nashville, TN: Thomas Nelson, 1997), pp. 137-38.

Chapter Seven: Keeping Our Vision Clear

1. C.S. Lewis, *Mere Christianity* (San Francisco, CA: HarperCollins Publishers, 1952), pp. 149-50.

2. Max Lucado, *No Wonder They Call Him the Savior* (Sisters, OR: Multnomah Publishers, 1986), p. 126.

Chapter Eight: Giving Up What Was Never Ours

1. Randy Alcorn, *The Treasure Principle* (Sisters, OR: Multnomah Publishers, 2001), p. 57.

2. Elizabeth George, *A Woman's Walk with God* (Eugene, OR: Harvest House Publishers, 2000), p. 172.

Chapter Nine: Radically Blessed

1. Bruce Wilkinson, *Set Apart* (Sisters, OR: Multnomah Publishers, 1998), p. 175.

Acknowledgments

To my wonderful husband, Art—God has used you in the most amazing ways to help me fulfill my purpose. Thank you for loving me, believing in me, supporting me, and fixing me hot chocolate on those late writing nights.

To the five most precious kids I know: Jackson, Mark, Hope, Ashley, and Brooke—Thank you for teaching me about God in our everyday adventures and for making our family such fun!

To Ron Graves—You'll never know how profoundly God changed my life the day you accepted my Bible.

To the staff of Proverbs 31 Ministries—Just like Moses had Aaron and Hur, I have you. Thanks for holding up my arms when I grow weary and for always being willing to come alongside me.

To Genia, Melanie, Marybeth, Holly, LeAnn, and Renee—Your never-ending encouragement is an oasis to me. Thank you for loving me and inspiring me to run the race strong.

To Terry, Carolyn, Barb, Kim, and the rest of the Harvest House family—Thank you for seeing this as more than a book and for sharing with me the impact it has made on each of you personally. This message would not be what it is without your editorial expertise and adventuresome vision.

About Lysa

Lysa TerKeurst is president of Proverbs 31 Ministries and the *New York Times* bestselling author of *The Best Yes, Unglued, Made to Crave,* and 16 other books.

As president of Proverbs 31 Ministries, Lysa and her team have led thousands to make their walk with God an invigorating journey through daily online devotionals, radio programs, online Bible studies, speaker/writing training, and more.

Lysa was recently awarded the Champions of Faith Author Award and has been published in multiple publications such as *Focus on the Family* and CNN online. Additionally, she has appeared on the *Today Show* as one of the leading voices in the Christian community.

Each year, Lysa is a featured keynote presenter at more than 40 events across North America, including the Women of Joy Conferences and the Catalyst Leadership Conference. She has a passion for equipping women to share their stories for God's glory through Proverbs 31 Ministries' annual She Speaks Conference and writer training program, COMPEL: Words That Move People.

Lysa's personal adventure of following God captured national media attention when their family adopted two teenage boys from a war-torn orphanage in Liberia, Africa. They never imagined their decision would start a chain reaction within their community, which inspired other families to adopt over 45 children from the same orphanage! Lysa's amazing story led to appearances on *The Oprah Winfrey Show, Good Morning America, The 700 Club, USA Today* newspaper, *Woman's Day* magazine, and *Focus on the Family* radio.

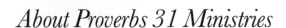

About Proverbs 31 Ministries

Lysa TerKeurst is the president of Proverbs 31 Ministries, located in Charlotte, North Carolina.

If you were inspired by *What Happens When Women Say Yes to God* and desire to deepen your own personal relationship with Jesus Christ, we have just what you're looking for.

Proverbs 31 Ministries exists to be a trusted friend who will take you by the hand and walk by your side, leading you one step closer to the heart of God through:

Free First 5 app
Free online daily devotions
Online Bible studies
Writer and speaker training
Daily radio programs
Books and resources

For more information about Proverbs 31 Ministries,
visit www.Proverbs31.org

To inquire about having Lysa speak at your event,
visit www.LysaTerKeurst.com and click on "speaking."

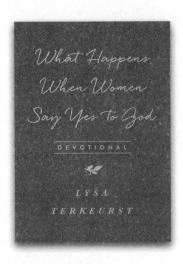

Keep Saying *Yes* to God Every Day

Let the important faith lessons from *What Happens When Women Say Yes to God* by Lysa TerKeurst inspire you daily through this 40-day devotional. Experience the joy and satisfaction of following God as you choose to say *yes* to all He has in store for you.

Each day you'll encounter scripture to ponder, a relatable story to encourage you, a prayer to help you put words to your desires, and a prompt to keep you moving forward.

When it comes to obeying God, a moment of perspective can stir your passion...and remind you that saying *yes* to Him is always the right path.

What Happens When Women Walk in Faith

LysaTerKeurst knows what it means to walk in faith, starting from the cry she uttered years ago, "How do I take my broken life and allow God to use it for His glory," to her current position as president of Proverbs 31 Ministry.

Walking in Faith will change the way you...

- recognize God's opportunities for growth
- hear God speak through His Word
- understand yourself as a unique creation of your heavenly Father
- survive life's hardest places

Filled with stories, Scripture, and encouragement, Lysa will help you discover the deeper truths of God. As a bonus, she provides a Bible study section to help you apply the principles in *Walking by Faith*.

More Lysa TerKeurst Books
from Harvest House Publishers

What Happens When Women Say Yes to God DVD

What Happens When Women Say Yes to God Interactive Workbook

What Happens When Young Women Say Yes to God

Am I Messing Up My Kids?

Other Great Reads
from Lysa TerKeurst

Finding I AM

Uninvited

The Best Yes

Becoming More Than a Good Bible Study Girl

Unglued

Made to Crave

Made to Crave for Young Women